TEACHING
—the sacred art

The *Joy* of
Opening Minds
& Hearts

Rev. Jane E. Vennard

Walking Together, Finding the Way®
SKYLIGHT PATHS®
PUBLISHING
Woodstock, Vermont

Teaching—The Sacred Art:
The Joy of Opening Minds and Hearts
2015 Quality Paperback Edition, First Printing
© 2015 by Jane E. Vennard

Library of Congress Cataloging-in-Publication Data
Available upon request.
ISBN 978-1-59473-585-1
ISBN 978-1-59473-597-4 (eBook)

10 9 8 7 6 5 4 3 2 1

Manufactured in the United States of America
Cover design: Jenny Buono
Cover art: Shutterstock/@Irishdesign

SkyLight Paths Publishing is creating a place where people of different spiritual traditions come together for challenge and inspiration, a place where we can help each other understand the mystery that lies at the heart of our existence.

SkyLight Paths sees both believers and seekers as a community that increasingly transcends traditional boundaries of religion and denomination—people wanting to learn from each other, *walking together, finding the way.*

SkyLight Paths, "Walking Together, Finding the Way" and colophon are trademarks of LongHill Partners, Inc., registered in the U.S. Patent and Trademark Office.

Walking Together, Finding the Way®
Published by SkyLight Paths Publishing
A Division of LongHill Partners, Inc.
Sunset Farm Offices, Route 4, P.O. Box 237
Woodstock, VT 05091
Tel: (802) 457-4000   Fax: (802) 457-4004
www.skylightpaths.com

For my students

Wisdom is a living stream, not an icon preserved in a museum. Only when we find the spring of wisdom in our own life can it flow to future generations.

—Thich Nhat Hanh

CONTENTS

Chapter Three

Love of Subject, Love of Learning: Communicating Excitement and Wonder

Chapter Four

Using Sacred Language: Telling Stories, Asking Questions, and Listening Well

Claiming Our Authority by Letting Go of Control

Attending to Our Inner Landscape: Seeing, Embracing, and Transforming Our Shadows

Teaching Who We Are:

INTRODUCTION

I come from a family of teachers. My maternal grandmother taught Greek and Latin in high school. My mother taught junior high math. My father was a college professor of engineering. Is it any wonder that I wanted nothing to do with teaching? I loved learning but never imagined myself on the other side of the desk. So how was it that I discovered that teaching was my calling, my vocation, my passion?

In my senior year of college I was aimless, not knowing what I would do after graduation. One day I saw a listing on a campus bulletin board announcing positions for teachers in the American School System, which runs schools all over the world for English-speaking students abroad. I was intrigued, not by the teaching opportunity but by the lure of travel.

I filled out the necessary paperwork and went for an interview, where they asked me where I would like to go. "Paris, Amsterdam, maybe Geneva," I replied.

"You and every other young woman," I was told. "But if you are willing to go where no one else wants to go, we can place you."

"Where might that be?" I asked.

"Taipei, Taiwan" was the reply. I agreed and then went home and looked it up on the map.

Eight months later I found myself in Tien Mou, a suburb of Taipei near an American military base, preparing a fourth-grade classroom for twenty-eight students. I was excited about the idea of teaching but was not prepared for the challenge ahead. I had taken a class in the philosophy of education and one in developmental psychology, neither of which were at all helpful. I had had no teacher training and knew nothing about lesson planning or classroom management.

It was a terrible year. Some mornings I would weep at the prospect of getting up and going back to the school. The students were out of control. They showed me no respect. Although I pushed them through the textbooks, gave spelling tests, and handed out math worksheets, no learning seemed to be taking place. All of us were miserable. I wondered how I might live through the second year of my contract.

When I was asked to teach during the summer, I reluctantly agreed, and this turned out to be a wise decision. Although I began that summer session with much trepidation, those six weeks gave me a positive experience of the teaching-learning process. I was given two small classes, one in remedial reading for third graders and the other in advanced math for middle schoolers. Both groups of students were motivated. The young ones really hoped to make progress, for they knew they were behind and wanted to catch up to their peers. The older students were intrigued with numbers and welcomed the opportunity to expand their natural ability through this special class.

In both classes I witnessed the students' struggle to learn, their willingness to keep trying, and then the excitement of mastering something new. I also began to grow in competence and confidence as I engaged the students in new ways. I learned how to pay attention to the children's needs, observe their different learning styles, and make adjustments in my teaching methods when necessary. I looked forward to each day, thinking not only about what I would teach, but also about what I might learn about the art of teaching. The highlight of that summer was when a little boy came up to me, holding a book, his eyes wide with wonder. "Guess what," he cried out. "All these words mean something!"

My second year was far better, although I realized how much I still needed to learn about teaching and learning. I applied for a master's program in education and upon my return to the United States immersed myself in study. What a wonderful year that was! Like my summer school students, I wanted to learn everything that was being taught. Upon graduation I was excited and ready to plunge into a new teaching position. I had found my vocation.

If you have picked up this book, you may have had a similar experience of stumbling into teaching and finding your vocation. Although some people feel called to teach from an early age, many others arrive at their vocation in more roundabout ways. Maybe you were in another field entirely but realized that when you were called to teach or mentor as part of your contract, excitement and eagerness rose within you. Maybe you were out of work when a friend asked you to help out in her preschool, and you found an unexpected joy in witnessing the little ones learn. Maybe you were asked to teach in the religious education program at your place of worship and you were amazed at the wonder of sharing your faith with people of many ages. You could be homeschooling your children and you realize every day the sacredness of your task.

You may not be or ever have been a teacher, but you are a lifelong learner. You remember with gratitude the wonderful teachers you have had, and you may be curious about how and why they were so effective. I wonder if the title of this book connecting the word *sacred* with the art of teaching caught your eye and something in your own life resonated with that idea. When teaching becomes a sacred art, it becomes a vocation.

TEACHING AS VOCATION

The women in my family did not teach long enough for teaching to become their passion. Although they both loved the profession, they had to stop teaching when they married—my grandmother because married women were not allowed to be teachers in the 1890s, and my mother because a household was expected to have only one family member employed during the early years of the Depression. My father, however, recognized his vocation when he became a teaching assistant during his master's program in engineering at MIT. I don't know whether he struggled as I did in his early years of teaching. I am not sure how he developed the confidence and determination that allowed him to turn down jobs in industry when he graduated in order to pursue a career in academia. I imagine that something in the teaching-learning process touched his heart and awakened his creativity.

In his early years of teaching at New York University, my father found no adequate textbook in his field of fluid mechanics. So he decided to write his own. Staying one week ahead of the class, he wrote the text in longhand, and then made it available to his students. When the textbook was published, he attracted the attention of the Stanford School of Engineering in Palo Alto, California, and was invited to join that faculty. Although many colleagues tried to dissuade him, we headed west in 1946.

In the twenty-three years before his death at the age of sixty, my father rose to full professor, rewrote his textbook four times, and taught and mentored thousands of young people. He not only stood before his students in the classroom but also worked alongside them in the huge laboratories where they could explore together the mysteries of flowing water. He turned down opportunities to become dean of the department, for he knew those responsibilities would take him away from the classroom.

Many years later, when my mother sold the house of our childhood, we gave away many of my father's things. In the subsequent years, after my mother died and my sister and I had moved from place to place, more items and books were left behind. I have only a few things remaining that belonged to my father—a plaque honoring his twenty-four years of teaching at the Stanford School of Engineering, the black-and-white VENNARD nameplate from his office door, a letter opener, and a dusty black book titled *The Art of Teaching*.

Published in 1951, this book now sits on my bookshelf. I discovered it a couple of years ago when my husband found it among our many books. I was glad to have it, but paid little attention to the title. I simply tucked it away with my other books and soon forgot about it. That book slipped back into my consciousness when I was considering writing this book on teaching for SkyLight Paths' Sacred Art series. "My father's book," I remembered, *The Art of Teaching*. Interestingly, I didn't rush to read it; I was simply aware of its presence. I began to see it with new eyes. I felt the connection to my father and our similar vocations. It seemed as if he was blessing my new project.

When I finally opened the book to read the introduction, I discovered why my father had cherished it. The author, Gilbert Highet, dismisses the idea that teaching is a science. He writes:

> Teaching involves emotions, which cannot be systematically appraised and employed, and human values, which are quite outside the grasp of science.... Teaching is not like inducing a chemical reaction: it is much more like painting a picture or making a piece of music; like

...g a garden or writing a friendly letter. You must throw your heart into it, you must realize that it cannot be done by formulas, or you will spoil your work, and your pupils, and yourself.[1]

THE HEART OF THE MATTER

Throwing ourselves fully into our teaching makes the experience vibrant and alive. With hearts open to our students, our material, and our own strengths and weaknesses, teaching becomes a sacred art. I have added the word *sacred* to the art of teaching not to view it as a religious calling but rather to bring to the profession a sense of reverence and respect. When something is sacred, it is set apart and deemed to be important and highly valued. I believe that teaching deserves such admiration.

When you bring that attitude of wonder into the classroom and meet your students with open hearts, you can see and treat all of them with respect. This does not mean you must love, or even like all of them, all the time. It is human to prefer one student over another, to have days when you feel as if you hardly care about any of them, or to wish that one particular student would drop your class. Paying attention to your inner experiences, recognizing and accepting those feelings, allows you to respond to your students with respect and compassion and see them clearly as individuals with their own life stories.

When our hearts are connected to our material and we treat the content of our teaching with awe, the subject matter is exciting. If we do not love our content, teaching and learning quickly become boring and dry. I had a high school teacher who taught United States history each year from the same notes. What I learned that year was that history was of little interest and had no relevance to my life.

I imagine you can remember at least one of your teachers who seemed to be disconnected from the subject and the students. Some might have seemed to be disconnected from life itself. I hope you have also had teachers whose hearts were in their teaching. What was it like to be in their classrooms, studios, or offices? Did they motivate and encourage you, even in the most challenging situations?

Not wanting to become bored or boring, I left the elementary school classroom after six years, not because I had lost my passion for teaching but because I began to find the subject matter of little interest. Fractions, insects, geography, and spelling were intriguing at first, for these subjects challenged me to find the most creative ways to help the children learn. But they began to lose their luster after a while.

Similarly, after teaching teachers for a number of years about classroom management, self-esteem, and gender inequity in our schools, I lost interest in that as well. I had no desire to keep up with new research in these fields. Now that I am teaching classes in prayer and spiritual formation, I feel continually challenged and creative. My love for the subject is clear to the students and increases their desire to learn. I realized the connection between my pleasure in the material and the learning experience in my early years of teaching when I asked my sixth-grade students their favorite subjects during the year. They overwhelmingly named poetry and mapmaking. At first I was puzzled, but then I understood. Those were two of the subjects I most loved to teach!

Besides our respect for students and our love of our subject and the very process of teaching and learning, we as teachers need to pay attention to who we are—our motivations, prejudices, feelings, strengths, and limitations. Our inner lives inform the ways we teach and how we treat our students. If we always focus outward, we may miss the richness of our own minds and hearts. Over my many years in classrooms with elementary school–age children, parents and teachers, seminary students and church leaders, I have discovered that in many ways I teach who I am. By our very presence, our responses to students and the environment, we are teaching important lessons. We may be teaching students to compete or cooperate by the way we manage our classroom. How we claim authority can teach students how to manipulate and control others, or how to use our power to empower others. When we make a mistake and apologize, we are teaching how to learn from our mistakes, rather than modeling ways to avoid them.

As you look back over your many years as a student in a variety of situations and settings, which classes, subjects, or teachers stand out? I know that Mrs. Rust taught me long division in the fifth grade, but mostly I remember her dignity, her respect for differences, her willingness to gently confront our bad behavior, her patience and good humor. I believe she knew exactly what she was teaching. She was teaching her subject matter through the clarity of who she was. She was teaching with integrity.

THE TEACHING LIFE

This book is about the teaching life—the messiness, wonder, joys, and frustrations. It is about the real day-to-day responsibility teachers have for their students. Although I have written this book primarily for people at all levels of the teaching profession, I recognize that authentic teaching goes on in a variety of settings. Parents are our earliest teachers, and many of these stories and ideas apply to raising children. In addition, the opportunity for sacred teaching and learning can be found in corporations, religious congregations, work sites, cafes and bars, sports fields, and prisons. I invite you to look at all the teaching-learning possibilities that exist in your life, not only your experiences in classrooms.

This is not a how-to book, and it contains little advice. Rather, it paints a broad picture of the teaching experience and invites you, the reader, to learn from the stories of others and to remember your own stories. Every chapter offers reflections and activities designed to draw you inward to learn from your own experiences. This inner exploration will guide you in understanding how your hopes and fears, joys and frustrations, gifts and limitations influence the realities that you face every day.

Many of you may be teaching in less than ideal situations. Our schools and institutions of higher learning are struggling with lack of funding; mandates for standardized testing; waning support from the community; and conflicts among administrators, teachers, and staff. The methods of teaching you would like to practice may not be welcome in your school. Your class size could make some activities impossible. You may be worn out and discouraged. You may be thinking of leaving your job. You may wish that the institution in which you teach could be reformed and transformed.

I think many teachers, parents, students, and administrators harbor that same hope. I know I do. But this is not a book about educational theory or how to create better schools. Instead, it is an invitation to look inward to your own motivations, the choices you have in the situation where you find yourself, and your desire to bring the exciting process of teaching and learning to the students you face each day. We do not teach in a perfect world, and energy spent on wishing it were different will not serve us or our students. My hope is that the stories and ideas in the following chapters will help you reconnect to your original desire to teach and inspire you to do what you can with what you have—to be realistic about your circumstances while at the same time reconnecting to your passion for your vocation, your students, and your subject, thus recognizing how teaching is a sacred art.

The first chapter explores the call to the teaching life. Using a number of stories from a diverse group of teachers, I recount how some felt called to teach from a very early age; others took a job and discovered their vocations; and still others realized their desire to teach later in life and had the courage to leave other jobs or careers to answer that call.

The next two chapters focus on respecting our students and engaging our subject matter, which, together with our love of learning, interact to support the teaching-learning process. We will look at three classroom models defined by what is central to the process—teacher-centered learning, student-centered learning, and subject-centered learning—and reflect on how each model has its place in different settings and with different students.

Chapter 4 continues this discussion by examining what I call sacred language. Sacred language is personal, questioning, metaphorical, and open. When teachers use forms of this language to communicate with students, learning connects to lived experience. Silence and listening are integral parts of sacred language. Our silence indicates our willingness to wait for ideas to spring forth, to step out of the way of a student's creative process, and to listen with our hearts to each student's needs and fears.

The teacher's authority and responsibility are the subject of Chapter 5. Although we may come to enjoy an easy relationship with our students as we share sacred language, we must remember our responsibility as the one in charge. When I asked my fifth graders to think about who was responsible for their learning, one student immediately responded, "You are 'cause you get paid!" Although I was hoping to help them see that learning was a shared responsibility, there was truth in what this child said. I might not be 100 percent responsible, but I had to be in charge. I set the emotional tone of the classroom, I chose the methods I thought best to meet the needs of the students, and I was called on to evaluate their progress. Claiming our authority in any classroom of children, teenagers, or adults is an integral part of the sacred art of teaching.

How to become aware of our inner lives is the topic of Chapter 6. Exploring our interior landscape helps us to recognize disappointments, unrealistic expectations, hidden prejudices, and insecurities. These issues need to be examined or they may keep us from claiming our authority, prevent us from being kind, or protect us from failure. In my teaching assignment right after graduate school, I noticed that I was overreacting to unexpected occurrences. When I looked within, I realized that I was terrified of losing control in the classroom, as I had so many times in my difficult year of teaching in Taiwan. Admitting the pain of that year, I could let go of the fear and remind myself that that experience was long ago and did not need to dominate my current teaching assignment. This awareness allowed me to relax into the present moment, teach the students who were before me, and welcome the surprises that would surely come. As you explore these traps or detours, remember that they are a natural part of the process of discovering who you are. By recognizing and acknowledging them, you will learn more about your vulnerabilities and strengths. Each exploration will take you deeper into your own self-knowledge and enable your teaching to become a sacred art.

The last chapter will examine more fully the idea that we teach who we are. To teach who we are, we must know where we come from, who we are, and who we are becoming. American mythologist Joseph Campbell wrote, "The privilege of a lifetime is being who you are."[2] The earlier chapters, with their reflection questions at the end, are designed to help you focus on these issues of identity before you get to this final chapter. Here we will take time to explore the inner landscape more intentionally, to help you discover a new freedom in your teaching and your living.

The stories throughout the book come from formal interviews, recollections of others in casual conversation, and my own experiences and memories over a lifetime of learning and teaching. The stories are filled with the love of teaching as well as acknowledging, in the words of teacher and poet Garret Keizer, "the impossibilities of teaching and the daily injustices it lays bare."[3]

People whose real names are used have given their permission. The others have been given pseudonyms or have been left unnamed. Certain details of the stories have been altered to protect identities. The memories that have flowed from my heart and mind are rendered as accurately as possible. May you find that these stories evoke your personal experiences and guide you to a deeper understanding of your own teaching life.

CHAPTER ONE

CALLED TO TEACH
DISCOVERING OUR VOCATION

I knew in my heart I was a teacher.

Erika Walker

Erika Walker grew up in a pioneering family on the eastern prairie of Colorado. She spent much of her childhood alone, exploring the natural world. Erika was fascinated with everything she encountered and longed to share her love of the world with others. She dreamed of becoming a rural schoolteacher, guiding her band of students into experiences and adventures that would open their minds and hearts.

After high school, Erika decided to honor her pioneering spirit by leaving her Colorado home to attend college in Florida. She majored in child psychology and education. Because of the courses she chose, she finished with an undergraduate degree but had no teaching credential. When she returned to Colorado, Erika entered a master's program in education, still holding her dream of becoming that creative, spontaneous teacher.

Erika became discouraged after just one quarter. She realized the classes she would need to take to complete her master's degree were uninspiring and were not going to prepare her for the kind of educational career she had imagined for herself. She confided in a friend her longing to teach in a way that included the whole world, where she could follow her students' interests, and together they would learn what they needed to know. Her friend painted a very different picture of what she was headed for with a teaching certificate. She described children seated in assigned rows, a structured curriculum with all students on the same page, and an overall goal of measuring progress. Erika was horrified. Although she had a taste of this reality in the first quarter of the program, it had never been stated with such clarity. With her dream of teaching turned into an image of a factory, she dropped out of the master's program. Had she abandoned her calling?

Jungian analyst James Hollis writes that the word *vocation* comes from the Latin word *vocatus*, or the calling to which the soul summons us. "We may choose careers," he writes, "but we do not chose vocation. Vocation chooses us."[1] A true vocation does not die, although it may go underground due to disappointment, obstacles, or interference from the circumstances of life. This is what happened to Erika.

"I lost the dream for a while," she told me. "I got very practical and decided to get an MBA." After completing that degree, she took a variety of jobs that paid her bills but realized that she was "working against her heart."

Eventually she ended up in a job where she counseled women who wanted to start their own businesses. She enjoyed guiding and mentoring her clients; however, she found the information she was offering them of little interest. But her longing to teach returned as she discovered ways to translate the dry material into something the women could learn and value. In one of these sessions, her young client exclaimed with great excitement, "In my heart I know I am a merchant!" Immediately Erika responded, "In my heart I know I am a teacher!" She had rediscovered her vocation, although it now looked nothing like her childhood dream. Her call to teach began to manifest in a variety of opportunities in colleges, churches, and not-for-profit organizations. Her most recent position is chair of the board of an environmental organization, where she is discovering and engaging teaching possibilities everywhere.

Erika's story illuminates some of the qualities that many teachers possess as they claim their teaching vocation. Erika was willing to listen to the guidance of her heart, even when she was not sure where she was headed. She was not afraid to step out of her comfort zone and take risks. When she found herself in situations where the use of her gifts was not obvious, she was able to see possibilities lurking in corners. Erika was creative in shaping her own life. All these qualities helped her stay connected to her original call.

LISTENING FOR THE CALL

Erika heard her call at a very young age, but most of the teachers I spoke with heard it much later in life and in a variety of settings. Steve Replogle never considered becoming a teacher. His mother, with whom he had a challenging relationship, was a teacher, and the last thing he imagined was following in her footsteps.

After he left college, he held a variety of jobs. Some were fun, and allowed him to both pay his bills and play at life. When Steve married and they had a child, he searched for and found more stable work. Some of the jobs were fulfilling, while others helped his new family become financially secure. But none of them seemed to fit who he was and who he was becoming. Steve wasn't sure where he belonged.

When Steve's daughter went to kindergarten, he began volunteering in her classroom, initially only one or two days a week, but he soon found he was eager to volunteer almost every school day. He realized he had a lot to offer children, that being with the little ones seemed natural, and he was having fun. "I am not sure I was called to teach," he told me. "I was drawn in, I couldn't resist. I actually felt that fate was at work."

Steve went back to school for a master's degree in education and a teaching certificate, became an elementary public school teacher at the age of thirty-eight, and has now been teaching the fourth grade in a public school for almost twenty years. Because he finds much about public education these days oppressive, he often considers leaving the classroom, but decides to keep going. "I want to be here with the kids," he told me.

Even though Erika and Steve have very different call stories and their own ways of living out their vocations, they share a similar theme. Both were aware when the work they were doing was not satisfying, and for some reason did not fit who they were. They were doing good work but not their soul work. They longed to be somewhere else but were not sure where that was. Yet

"When the spirit within you is unhappy at being confined, it can compel you to lead a true and authentic life."

the prompting to go toward the unknown was there within them. Spiritual teacher Adyashanti puts it this way: "When the spirit within you is unhappy at being confined, it can compel you to lead a true and authentic life."[2] That life of integrity and vitality for both Erika and Steve came in the form of teaching.

HEARING AND LIVING THE CALL

Peter Baer, a high school English teacher, was also guided into recognizing his vocation by first realizing what he didn't want to do. Peter was a philosophy major at the University of California at Berkeley. He was in love with ideas and passionate about social justice. He thought he might earn a doctorate in the philosophy of education and through research in the academy contribute to structural changes in public schools that would help the most underserved students succeed.

But Peter recognized the "ivory tower syndrome," where professors lecture about education without ever setting foot in a public school classroom. They lack credibility with those preparing to teach. Therefore he found a master's program at Stanford University that the state of California would fund if he agreed to teach in a low-performing, low-income California school for four years after graduation. Although he still believed he was ultimately headed for the world of academia, he decided to sign the agreement to see where it would lead.

After graduating from the program, he took a position in Alameda, California, at a very economically diverse high school. After five years he moved to a high school in Richmond, California, where 98 percent of the students came from families at or below the poverty level. By that time Peter was hooked. "I realized teaching was my vocation, not because I experienced a call but because I felt I was perfectly suited to the classroom. It was natural. It fit." Although he has changed schools several times in his twelve years of teaching, he is always drawn to neighborhoods where he interacts with disadvantaged young people he believes can most benefit from his gifts. When I asked him if he ever thought about leaving the classroom to return to academia, he told me that during the really tough times it sounded appealing. Then he added, "But it breaks my heart to think of not seeing those passionate, frustrating, evolving, and ridiculous teenagers every day."

While their calls to teach and their roles are different from one another, Erika, Steve, and Peter have discovered a passion for teaching. Best-selling author and international speaker Sr. Joan Chittister places passion at the center of the experience of vocation. "Passion," she writes, "both stretches us beyond ourselves and deepens us within at the same time."[3] That stretching seems clear in all three of these stories.

Peter was stretched beyond his original vision for himself when he let go of his idea of becoming an academic whose research into the systems of education could change the world. Rather, he found himself in the chaos of a high school classroom

"Being a high school teacher is now deeply ingrained in my identity."

where his presence would impact the personal worlds of his students. "I have grown into myself through the day-to-day experiences of the classroom," he said. "Being a high school teacher is now deeply ingrained in my identity."

Erika was stretched as she faced the truth that her original dream of teaching was never going to be realized. In her disappointment, she chose a more practical career in business. Although she knew that business was not her calling, she tapped into a depth of creativity within herself to find ways and means to teach in the midst of any position she held.

Steve's call stretched him beyond an earlier rejection of his family. His experience in his daughter's class wiped away his assumptions and moved him beyond his preconceived notions of who he was. He has also discovered during his many years of teaching that his success in the classroom and the awards he has received are nothing compared to the realization that his vocation is part of a bigger process. "Teaching has a religious dimension," he told me. "We are not solitary teachers doing our job. We are connected to each other and to God, creating something more than any one of us could do alone."

While Erika, Steve, and Peter felt called to teach and discovered a passion for the teaching-learning process, that does not mean they are not ambivalent about their role. Teaching is hard work. The educational systems in which we work are often oppressive and less than encouraging and supportive. Values and personalities clash and lead to conflict. The demands and expectations placed upon teachers can seem overwhelming. Both Steve and Peter admitted there were times they wanted to leave. When I asked Joey, a Montessori teacher you will meet in Chapter 3, whether he ever thought about leaving the classroom, he replied, "Every day!"

"There was never a time during the sixteen years I taught when I didn't imagine doing something else," wrote high school English teacher and poet Garret Keizer. "I would begin the year with a burst of enthusiasm accompanied by the fervent hope that come June I'd be done with teaching for good."[4] He did finally leave the classroom to follow his call to write, but after fourteen years returned to teach for one year. This allowed him to reflect realistically on the tension between his call to teach and his equally strong call to write. I imagine this ambivalence about vocation is shared by many of us.

VOCATION IN RELIGIOUS SETTINGS

In the Roman Catholic tradition, the idea of vocation has always had a narrow and specific meaning. A vocation was understood to mean that you were called by God to be a priest or a nun. You were being asked to give your life to God and to the church. Catholic families were honored if one or more of their children had a vocation to the religious life. This understanding of vocation remains today. Faithful Catholics are encouraged to pray for "more vocations" as the priesthood shrinks and fewer women are joining convents.

The Protestant tradition similarly uses the term *call* to mean an invitation to become ordained to the Christian ministry. In my denomination, the United Church of Christ, the call to ministry is understood to be not only a call from God but also a call from the people, the gathered community of the church, which provides an opportunity for an individual's call to be validated. The term *call* can also be used in the question, "What is your call?" or the statement "I have received a call."

All this terminology was new to me when I entered seminary to explore my Christian heritage. When a fellow student asked me about my call, I didn't know what he was talking about. I later learned that what he was wondering was how I was planning to serve the church—through parish ministry, youth ministry, a ministry of music, or maybe a hospital chaplaincy. I had no idea. The only honest answer I could give was this: "I have been called to seminary."

When a weekend retreat on "Exploring Your Call" was offered, I eagerly signed up for it. I wanted to reflect on who or what was calling me, what it meant to be called, where this seminary journey might lead me. I liked the idea of reflecting on these puzzling issues in community. Much to my surprise and disappointment, the weekend turned out to be instructions on how to get a job after graduation from seminary. We were given guidelines for filling out applications, received information on the necessary paperwork, and were encouraged to settle on what kind of position we were seeking. Since I was still unclear about my call, I was disappointed that the retreat had ended up as more of a job fair than the spiritual experience I had anticipated.

CALL AS SPIRITUAL JOURNEY

As you can tell from my story and the stories of others, I have moved from a narrow religious use of the words *call* and *vocation* but have not excluded the possibility of its spiritual dimensions. In the words of memoirist Shirley Hershey Showalter, from her book *Blush*: "The calling to be a teacher wasn't some magic wand of authority one waved. Like all callings, it would be a spiritual journey."[5] In other words, a call is an invitation to discover our vocation, to become what and who we are meant to be.

In a religious context, receiving a call assumes that God is involved, but many people with no belief in God use the term as well. They may believe their call is coming from their soul or an inner wisdom. Maybe it comes from our higher self or our true self. Sometimes it is heard as a longing, or a prompting that comes from deep within. Wherever the call originates, there are many ways people describe recognizing that call.

Erika heard her call by seeing an image of herself as a teacher. Steve heard his with the felt sense of being drawn into teaching. Peter heard his call after arriving in a high school classroom and, through those four years, recognizing he was where he belonged.

Some people hear a call that is loud and clear and they move directly toward their vocation. Others report the call as a still, small voice that beckons them from the silence. Occasionally the call is insistent, and other times it gently comes and goes. Often the call is puzzling, leaving the hearer confused about what to do. When St. Francis of Assisi, a twelfth-century monk, heard God call him to repair the church, he thought he was supposed

"The calling to be a teacher wasn't some magic wand of authority one waved. Like all callings, it would be a spiritual journey."

to fix the little run-down chapel in the town of Assisi. Only later did he understand that he was being called to reform the Catholic Church of his day, saving it from the sins of greed and oppression.

Whenever and however we hear a call, it is wise to pay attention to it. With reflection we may discover that it is not from the soul, but rather from some other place within us. Maybe we are bored with our life and we just want to try something different. It could be that we are responding to old family messages telling us what we "should" do. To sort through these voices and discern the authenticity of a call, you may need a trusted friend, or a group of friends, who can gently question your motivations and feelings in response to your call. This was the process for a young man in the Episcopal Church who felt called to the priesthood. In that tradition, when individuals experience a call, they are required to gather a committee to help them discern whether each one is truly called to become a priest.

His committee met with him for eight months in an atmosphere of prayer for questions, reflection, and dialogue. Over time he came to realize that he had heard the call to the priesthood at a time when he was dissatisfied with his corporate job. In his frustration and unhappiness, he looked around to see what other options might be available. As an active lay member of his congregation, he had always seen and admired the ministries of the priests. He began to think that becoming a priest was what he was called to do.

By the end of the discernment process, however, he came to realize that his true call was to stay in his present job and make changes in himself and in his role that would lead to more creativity and satisfaction, and could possibly help change the culture of the organization. "My call was to a more

authentic and purposeful life just where I was," he said grate-
fully at the last meeting of his committee. "Not a call to the
priesthood."

AN AUTHENTIC CALL

Joan Chittister outlines her understanding of an authentic
call as something that fits our skills, something that goes
beyond either interest or ability, and something that drives
us beyond both talent and passion to a sense of purpose.[6]
Although every authentic call may not fit this description
exactly, we can see echoes of her guidelines in the stories of
Erika, Steve, and Peter. We also see it clearly in the example
of the man who entered the discernment process to consider
what he thought was his call to the priesthood. His true call,
as he came to recognize, was to remain in his current position where he could use his skills. This realization drove him
beyond his desire to escape, and ultimately fulfilled his longing for a purposeful life.

I believe we receive many authentic calls in life, not just
one with a clear vocation as a result. Looking back, we can
likely see a pattern in how our different calls have led us, frequently on a circuitous path, to embrace a vocation that will
manifest in a variety of ways over time. In my own story my
longing to travel did not prove to be an authentic call but simply the desire for adventure that was entirely appropriate for
that time of my life. From my teaching experience in Taiwan,
I received an authentic call to make teaching my vocation.
This call came from my experience and deepened over time
through my master's degree program and subsequent years
of teaching. When I left the elementary classroom to teach
adults, I was not experiencing a new call, but rather an expan-
sion of my vocation as a teacher that stretched me beyond
myself and deepened my sense of self as a teacher.

So imagine my surprise when I experienced another authentic call, a summons to attend seminary. I had started practicing Zen Buddhist meditation and felt very connected to the tradition. My call came while sitting in meditation in a Buddhist community. I heard a gentle "voice" telling me that the Buddhist tradition was a beautiful tradition but it was not mine. I interpreted this awareness as a call to delve into my Christian roots. Not sure at first how to do that, I soon decided to go to seminary, an idea that had never before entered my mind. But the call included many dimensions of authenticity. Exploring Christianity in an academic setting fit my skills of study and learning, it certainly went beyond my current interests of designing and teaching continuing education classes, and I was surprised to realize it carried with it a sense of purpose. I was being called out from my comfort zone into the unknown.

Attending seminary did not take me on a path away from my teaching vocation, but broadened my teaching venues to include churches, retreat centers, and seminaries. Later the invitation to write came in the form of a phone call from an editor who had heard me speak about intercessory prayer. She invited me to work with her on a project that would include my writing a book on how to pray for others. Since I would be writing what I had been teaching, this opportunity felt like an integral part of my original call and my teaching vocation.

If you look back over your own winding way to the place you find yourself today, I can imagine that, although different from mine, your journey may reflect the truth that we do not choose our vocations. Vocation chooses us. And chooses us. And chooses us. The faithful task is to listen to the call, discern and respond, and perhaps let go of the life we had planned in order to risk embracing the new life that awaits us.

RISKY BUSINESS

Heidi Boerstler says that the most important factor in finding her vocation was her willingness to take risks. She had to listen to her inner wisdom and trust that following its guidance would lead her to where she needed to be. At age twenty she gave birth to a severely disabled daughter and her eyes were opened to the need to fight for people with no voice. She did not experience this as a call to teaching, but rather as a call to study, to learn what was needed to make the world a better place. She earned a doctorate in public health and followed that with a law degree. One of her early jobs was as an accountant in a health care agency. She found accounting tedious, but the opportunity arose for her to teach the agency's clients how to manage their own accounts. That was her first taste of teaching and it felt natural, like finding herself at home in her own skin.

Vocation chooses us. And chooses us. And chooses us.

With this experience she set out for a career in higher education, and was hired as a research instructor at the University of Colorado School of Business. She was stretched into new fields, risked taking assignments that she was not sure she could succeed at, and in the process learned more and more about herself as a teacher. She is now a tenured full professor at the business school, teaching a course she designed titled Health Law, Ethics, and Transformational Leadership.

Although not a religious person, Heidi is deeply spiritual, and her spiritual practices are the foundation of her course design and her teaching. She has written her own textbooks and a workbook that invites her graduate students to look within, to connect their heads and their hearts, and to ask themselves important questions about meaning, purpose, and service. "I do not use spiritual language in my teaching or writing," she acknowledged. "I need to translate those ideas into language familiar to my students, colleagues, and administrators. I trust that those who are ready will hear a deeper message."

Heidi's courses are well attended and well reviewed. She was recently asked to produce a promotional video for the business school. As I watched this short piece, I was struck by her skill in conveying the necessary factual information while at another level appealing to the hearts of prospective students. She feels that she is in the right place at the right time, doing what she loves, and she is deeply grateful. She sums up her understanding of call and vocation by exclaiming, "It's all about listening and staying awake to the opportunities that arise, then choosing to risk flinging yourself into the unknown, trusting you will end up exactly where you need to be to bring goodness into the world."

> "It's all about listening and staying awake to the opportunities that arise, then choosing to risk flinging yourself into the unknown."

CALLED TO A PURPOSEFUL LIFE

Letting go of how you thought your life might be, having the courage to take risks, and experiencing passion for what you are doing is not the whole story of call and vocation. Joan Chittister reminds us that a true call drives us beyond all these things to a sense of purpose. Answering your call is not just for you to lead a life of fullness and vitality. Discovering your vocation is about sharing your gifts and being of service in the world.

Erika serves the world by sharing her creativity and love of learning in various organizational settings. Peter serves his high school students by challenging them with ideas and his commitment to justice. He believes in his students and through his words and actions helps these young people believe in themselves. Steve says his purpose is to share with his fourth-grade students the books, art, and poetry he loves and takes to heart. Heidi's purpose is to offer to her graduate students who are pursuing a career in business the idea that a life of the spirit would not be antithetical to their chosen profession. "I don't think many of them have ever before considered that possibility," she said.

Mark Sisun believes his original call was to service, rather than to teaching. For many years he answered that call through the practice of law, working for justice within the legal system. Because of the stress of his profession, he learned to meditate and began practicing yoga. He found in these practices a new way of life, and felt a desire to study these traditions more deeply. He eventually closed his large law firm and moved it to a much smaller office where, instead of litigating cases, he could consult with and supervise other attorneys, thus giving him time to pursue his passion.

After studying extensively for many years with a number of great yoga masters, Mark wanted to share some of what he had learned so that others could also benefit from the knowledge and experiences he had acquired. "I believe I have an obligation to pass on what I had learned on mat and cushion," he explained. Soon he began offering yoga classes at a local health club. He works with students at all levels of ability, often in the same class, offering clear instructions and reminding those in attendance not to strive for perfection, but rather to listen to their bodies as they literally and figuratively unfold. "Seeing the changes over months, watching these bodies and minds opening like flowers, warms my heart," he said.

His students tell me Mark is a natural teacher who challenges and encourages them at the same time. His words are clear and not cluttered with more information than is necessary. He is teaching mindfulness as well as yoga postures, and mixes the two easily. He reminds his students to keep listening to their bodies, breathe into the poses, and notice what happens.

My husband, Jim, who was at first uncertain as to whether he would fit into Mark's yoga class, now goes gladly twice a week. "I think I am still the oldest and least flexible person there," he said. "But that doesn't matter anymore. Mark is able to make us all comfortable at the same time he challenges us with his gentle instructions." Jim is noticing subtle changes in his body as well as an opening of his awareness to the world around him. Mark's call to serve is being lived out as he shares with others what he knows, loves, and lives.

Mark, along with the other teachers in this chapter, heard a call and came to their vocations not by striving but by listening. This does not negate the hard work that was involved in all these stories, but that effort was more about surrender and risk taking than it was about pushing forward. The Buddhists call this "effortless effort," which I believe sums up what it means to be called and to respond. Our vocation arrives, not through our own willfulness but as a gift to be received with grateful hearts.

Looking Inward, Going Deeper

1. What is your "call" story? I invite you to draw your story. This picture can simply be a line. Notice where the line is straight and when it curves or changes direction abruptly. You may make note of when you lost your way or indicate the different choices you made at different times of your life. Try not to judge; simply draw your journey and let the image speak to you. What does it reveal?

2. How have your call and vocation stretched you beyond an image of yourself into a new way of being and living in the world and to a more authentic sense of purpose?

3. What risks were involved in responding to your call? Do you resonate with Heidi's experience of flinging yourself into the unknown? What words might you use to describe your understanding of call and vocation?

4. Are you feeling discouraged as you read these stories, which are filled with passion and purpose? Do you long for the vibrancy they express, rather than thinking of your teaching as simply your job? What might you learn from the lived experience of others that would help you reconnect to your original motivation to become a teacher?

CHAPTER TWO

ENGAGING OUR STUDENTS AND COLLEAGUES

RESPECT, CHALLENGE, AND KINDNESS

I set the bar high and expect great things from students and teachers alike.

Kristin Waters

When I went to South High School in Denver, Colorado, to speak with the principal, Kristin Waters, she was observing a teacher and students in an advanced physics class. Kristin spends most of her time in the halls and classrooms engaging the fourteen hundred students, along with an excellent group of teachers. She is a hands-on administrator and when I asked her what nourishes her soul in this setting, she replied, "My passion for the work and the people and the deep belief in what we are doing."

In her teenage years, Kristin taught swimming and was a counselor in a day camp, but had no thought of teaching.

After college she went to Europe for a year to serve as an au pair. When she returned, she realized that she needed to be in school and she never looked back. "I guess you might say that my feeling of urgency was a call," she said. Kristin applied for and received an emergency license to teach English and French in a junior high school in south Los Angeles while she studied for her teaching certificate.

Kristin later moved to a middle school in a neighboring district. As she spent more time in the classroom, she realized how much more of an impact she could have on the educational system as an administrator and enrolled in a master's program in administration. When she moved to Denver, she accepted a teaching position that led to an assistant principal position, where she began to cultivate her administrative talents. Soon after, she became principal of a middle school that was declining in enrollment, and after turning the school around was named principal of one of the most underachieving high schools in Colorado.

When Kristin improved student academic achievement and increased overall student performance in that school, she was called to the top administrative offices, first to oversee all charter and innovative schools, and then all the high schools in the district. She filled those positions for two years but longed to be back with the students and teachers and not one step removed from the daily activities of teaching and learning, as she was in her supervisory role.

Her present high school is doing well, but is not without its challenges. The student body has children from seventy countries, many of whom speak English as a second language. The school is mandated to provide for special needs of all sorts—cognitive, physical, and emotional disabilities, as well as offering programs for the gifted. "Teaching is exhausting work," she said. "Already this fall two of my faculty requested leaves of absence and one new teacher resigned."

Kristin is committed to teachers' well-being and continued commitment to their call. She provides faculty meetings where teachers can step back from the overwhelming details of the work to share successes, receive encouragement, and grieve over disappointing and sometimes tragic events with students and their families. "The grief inherent in the teaching life needs to be acknowledged and felt," she said. "Otherwise, we can't move forward."

Kristin has a deep belief in the inner strength, goodness, and

"The teacher kindles the light; the oil is already in the lamp."

knowledge within both teachers and students. She believes they want to do their best, grow in competency, and find joy in the teaching-learning process. By cultivating with her whole staff a safe and trusting environment, she draws out the wisdom of everyone engaged in the educational process.

HONORING STUDENTS' INNATE WISDOM

In our exploration of teaching as a sacred art, we need to remember that the root meaning of *educate* is to "draw out" or "call forth." Our students do not sit before us as blank slates to be written upon or as empty vessels waiting to be filled with our knowledge. Rather, they have their own life experience to draw on, their unique ways of knowing, their intuition, and their remarkable ability to figure things out for themselves. In the words of a traditional Sufi saying, "The teacher kindles the light; the oil is already in the lamp."[1]

When my friend Lynn was in the sixth grade, her teacher challenged the class with a question: "What number do you get when you divide zero by one?" The whole class quickly responded, "Zero!" "Does everyone agree?" he asked. Again a unanimous "Yes!" "All right, try this one. What do you get when you divide one by zero?" With little thought the class shouted, "Zero!" "Does everyone agree?" he asked. "No," said Lynn in a very small voice.

Lynn was sitting at her desk looking at the problem, thinking deeply. She knew it couldn't be zero but she couldn't find the words to say what she knew. Her teacher then asked her gently, "Do you want to change your answer, Lynn?" Frightened at the prospect of going against all of her classmates, she nonetheless summoned the courage to respond with another "no" and then went on to explain, "It can't be zero, but I don't know what it is. All I know is it is big, really big, as big as this," and she threw her arms wide. The class was stunned; her teacher smiled broadly. "Lynn is right," he said, "and the answer she is looking for is 'infinity.'"

In that seemingly simple exchange, Lynn found her authentic voice, her inner wisdom. Years later she went back to her teacher to tell him how important that day was in her life, for in that moment she realized she could trust her inner knowing, speak up against a majority, and be affirmed for her insight and courage. As she grew up, she returned to that moment as a touchstone when she sensed she knew something important and was searching for the courage to speak. Her teacher's respectful method of questioning the class had allowed Lynn's inner wisdom to come forth.[2]

Teacher and writer Parker J. Palmer, author of *The Courage to Teach*, calls this innate wisdom *the teacher within*, and applies it to both student and teacher. "We can speak to the teacher within our students," he writes, "only when we are on speaking terms with the teacher within ourselves."[3] He understands our inner teachers to be the voice of integrity, guiding us to our authentic selves.

Paul Baker, a professor of theater arts, named this innate wisdom "the god within—that creative self in everybody."[4] He goes on to say that he believes our creative self is spiritual and the spiritual task of teachers is to help their students recognize their inner wisdom and put it to work. When we believe that all students have within them this creative ability, even if we cannot see it, we can search for ways to elicit it.

Recognizing and honoring the inner wisdom in ourselves is vital for teachers as well. When we look behind our lesson plans and under our performing selves to discover our authentic selves, we can model this inner process for our students. We need to look for and discover our own creative abilities and put them to work in our teaching and our lives.

I remember an incident, while I was a student in high school, where the wisdom and creative ability of both teacher and students were revealed. We were studying poetry, and our teacher was taking us line by line through a poem. With great authority, he explicated the structure, images, and metaphors and told us exactly what the poet was trying to convey through his words. At the end of a long explanation of the deep meaning of the poem, one student raised her hand. "How do you know what the poet means?" she asked bluntly. "You didn't write this poem. I think we each have to figure out for ourselves what the words mean."

After a shocked silence, Mr. Vittetoe put aside his lesson plans and said, "So let's figure it out." There ensued a lively discussion of what the poem meant to each student, how the images spoke differently to individuals. We discovered that there could be no right or wrong way to read this poem; we had to recognize how it touched our minds and hearts. I don't remember the poem under discussion, but I do remember how Mr. Vittetoe helped us struggle with what the poem meant to each of us, calling forth our own wisdom and guiding us not only to a new way of reading poetry but also to a new way of thinking about learning.

All of us have strengths and weaknesses in our learning abilities—areas where we excel and areas we tend to avoid because they are difficult for us. When both students and teachers experience their own inner wisdom, they become more open to new information, difficult ideas, and different fields of study. They are more willing to explore subjects and information they are not drawn to.

As we respect the inner wisdom, the creative self, in all students, we also need to be aware that their wisdom will emerge in different ways and in different areas of learning. Lynn discovered her voice in an arithmetic lesson. Poetry was the avenue that released the inner wisdom of the student asking a heartfelt question in Mr. Vittetoe's class. Other students may be surprised by their own inner wisdom in areas such as music, art, or dance. These differences we see in our students are an indication that intelligence is experienced and manifested in a variety of ways. When we become aware of this, it is much easier to respect our individual students for their wisdom and uniqueness.

DISCOVERING MULTIPLE INTELLIGENCES

When I first encountered Howard Gardner's theory of multiple intelligences in his 1983 book *Frames of Mind*,[5] I thought excitedly, "So *that's* what's been going on in my classrooms!" Gardner asserted that, rather than intelligence being a single entity that can be measured with IQ tests, there are a number of forms of intelligence that allow people to resolve genuine problems or difficulties within certain cultural settings. His research and study led him to posit seven intelligences that satisfied his criteria for calling a particular ability an intelligence. The seven that qualified were linguistic, mathematical,

musical, spatial, body/kinesthetic, and the personal intelligences that include both interpersonal and intrapersonal
intelligence.

These intelligences are often described in terms of behaviors, skills, or particular awareness. Linguistically intelligent
people have a way with words. They love to read, write, and
play word games. When I read that one of the behaviors of linguistically intelligent people
is to read dictionaries, I was
amazed. I did that a lot and
never told anyone because I

*"So that's what's been going
on in my classrooms!"*

thought it was weird. Mathematical intelligence shows up in a
facility with numbers as well as abstract ideas. When my older
stepson was asked how he arrived at a solution to a complex
mathematical problem, he couldn't tell us. "I just see it," he
said.

Musical intelligence is often observed in children as they
gravitate toward musical instruments, make up tunes, and
respond actively to rhythms. You are spatially intelligent if
you have a good sense of direction, can easily read a map,
and have an inclination to straighten framed photos and wall
hangings in other people's offices and homes. You may also
have a talent for artistic expression, and may notice that you
learn more easily when you are given an image or a diagram
to help you understand a concept. History opened up to me
when a skilled teacher introduced us to time lines in her world
history class.

People with body/kinesthetic intelligence want to move,
dance, build, and touch the world around them. They are
unusually adept at both large and small motor skills and
often graceful in their movement. Those with high personal
intelligences are able to look into the heart of things. Inter-
personally intelligent individuals have an aptitude for people

skills. They know how to mediate a conflict, bring people together, and listen sympathetically to another's problems. They can often sense what another person is feeling, so they are naturally empathetic. Intrapersonally intelligent people have a rich inner life. They may delve into the meaning of their dreams, and seek out people who will help them gain self-knowledge.

Over the years I had seen these many intelligences exhibited in students of all ages, but had no way to name or explain what I perceived. If you are a parent, haven't you witnessed these many intelligences in your children? Maybe your young son is a skilled peacemaker (interpersonal) in his classroom. Maybe your adolescent daughter can fix anything that is broken (spatial and body/kinesthetic) from the living room clock to the plumbing under the sink. And then there are those students of all ages who are amazingly self-aware (intrapersonal) of their feelings, motivations, and prejudices.

> Why are we alive? What does life mean? Why are there wars? What is love?

Since Gardner's original work, many people have suggested other intelligences beyond the original seven. Gardner at first was reluctant to alter his theory, but eventually he conceded that there might be two other intelligences that fit his criteria.[6] One is naturalist intelligence, which is the core capacity to distinguish the diverse characteristics in nature. The person with a strong naturalist intelligence can tell the difference between many similar plants, or look at the clouds and know what weather is coming.

The other intelligence that met Gardner's criteria was existential intelligence, which is the capacity to ponder the big questions of life: Why are we alive? What does life mean? Why are there wars? What is love?

These questions are asked by people of all ages. A five-year-old asked me, as I drove him home from the hospital where he had visited his mother and met his new baby brother, "Why him?" He was not asking about the process of birth, but rather the unanswerable questions of why this particular child, at this particular time, in this particular family. I have found that recognition of the multiple intelligences helps me show respect for the strengths and weaknesses of my students.

TEACHING TO MULTIPLE INTELLIGENCES

Paul Baker tells of a student in his theater class who was a gifted dancer, brilliant in rhythm, but was failing English. He suggested to the English teacher that she point out to the student and help him experience the rhythm inherent in the English language. When the young man began to experience the connection, he was able to transfer his giftedness to a subject other than dance.[7] Transferring gifts of one intelligence to promote learning in another area has been facilitated by teachers in all subjects and in all learning situations, whether they have ever heard of Gardner's work or not.

As we adapt our teaching methods to honor the different intelligences in the classrooms, we often become aware of ways individual students need special help in transferring their skills from one intelligence to another. A very creative high school history teacher had a student who was engaged in the material, had a lot of facts straight, and seemed to have a strong sense of the historical period being studied. Yet he continually failed the tests. Recognizing the body/kinesthetic and musical gifts of this star basketball player, the teacher took him after school to the basketball court and had him shoot baskets while he read the student the test questions. The young man answered enough questions correctly to pass the course.

Becoming aware of and respecting the different intelligences of your students is not enough. You would be wise to know the different ways you are intelligent, your strengths and your limitations, for teachers tend to teach to the intelligence in which they themselves excel. They forget, or never realized, that all students do not learn as they do.

This was a startling realization for religion and ethics professor Dana Wilbanks when he began teaching at the Iliff School of Theology in Denver, Colorado. From high school through college and into his PhD program, he had learned almost entirely from teachers giving lectures. When he began teaching, he simply taught as he had always been taught, crafting lectures to inform the students of the material he loved and knew so well. "It didn't take long," he told me, "to see that many of the students were not engaging me or the subject. The lecture method didn't work for them. I needed help."

> Teachers tend to teach to the intelligence in which they excel.

Dana taught the way he had learned. But from the other side of the desk he saw the need to speak to other intelligences, other ways of learning. He needed to discover ways to engage students of different intelligences. He turned to his colleagues for guidance and opened himself and his students to a variety of teaching methods. He began to pose current ethical questions to his students to reflect on and write about before the next scheduled class. Then he would invite them into small groups to share their reflections, looking for areas of agreement and disagreement. That preparation often led to lively discussions with most of the students taking part.

Even when teachers choose to teach the subject matter in their area of strength, they need to be aware of the other intelligences. If you are mathematically intelligent, you may be drawn to teaching math, but unless you are teaching a postgraduate course, you cannot assume that all your students have strong mathematical intelligence. They may need to take your class to satisfy a requirement for graduation, and find the material difficult to comprehend. They will need a variety of teaching methods to master the material.

The teacher's task is to engage other intelligences to help the students find their way in an area where they seem to have few gifts.[8] By crossing over lines that divide one form of intelligence from another, we are recognizing both the gifts and the limitations of our students. We are seeing them for who they are, rather than passing judgment about their abilities, allowing us to offer them deep respect.

RESPECT FOR THE STRUGGLE

Teachers tend to teach in areas in which they excel and students choose to pursue the subjects that are the easiest for them. However, students limit themselves when they refuse to explore areas where they have no natural ability. When I asked for piano lessons as a young child, I was told that it would be a waste of time and money because Vennards were not musical. To this day I have to summon great courage to proceed when I'm asked to perform anything musical. Since I did so well in other areas, I was not encouraged to struggle to learn something new and problematic.

When students only delve into subjects for which they have natural ability, they may begin to believe that all learning should come easily. If they encounter a difficult subject, they often turn away, for they have not learned to tackle new learning experiences. UCLA psychology professor Jim Stigler believes that our North American culture equates struggle with lack of ability, so that students avoid anything they find difficult. In addition, these students tend to give up more easily than students in other cultures when they are faced with a new problem or idea. For example, in Asian cultures, struggle indicates strength, and when students persevere they are rewarded.

Stigler witnessed the affirmation of struggle in a fourth-grade classroom in Japan. He sat in the back of the room as the teacher proceeded to teach the children to draw cubes. One of the students having trouble with the problem was invited to the front of the room to work on the board in view of his classmates. Every time the student tried to complete the task, the teacher would ask the class how he did. The other students would shake their heads and the boy at the board would try again.

Stigler reported how anxious this process made him, watching this youngster struggle and fail time after time. But when the boy finally got it right, and the teacher asked the students how he did this time, they broke into applause. The child returned to his seat beaming, proud of his achievement.[9]

In Asian cultures, Stigler concludes, teachers give assignments that stretch the student so they can experience the rewards of struggle. This rarely happens in North American classrooms. These cultural differences were highlighted in a study where first-grade students were given a math problem that could not be solved. The American students worked on the problem an average of thirty seconds, and then said, "We haven't had this." The Japanese students worked a full hour and the study coordinators had to stop the session.[10] Our teaching methods may never parallel those of the Japanese classroom, but we must be attuned to our own experiences of difficult learning situations. If we ourselves can't persevere when learning gets difficult, we will be uncomfortable watching our students struggle. We might be tempted to step in to rescue them, provide lessons that are easy, or be reluctant to challenge them with ideas and tasks that stretch them beyond their perceived capabilities.

Some teachers deliberately choose to teach in areas where they had difficulty as students. I have met reading teachers who had a hard time learning to read, and still find reading an effort in their adult lives. Because it has been a struggle for them, they believe they can bring a depth of understanding to the students in their classes. As one first-grade teacher told me, "So many people don't remember learning to read, they just remember always reading. Because they didn't struggle, it is hard for them to understand what the students are going through."

> We need to be mindful of how other students respond to one student's struggle.

We also need to be mindful of how other students respond to one student's struggle. Imagine what would have happened in the Japanese classroom if the boy at the board had been teased, laughed at, or otherwise disrespected. If we are to support students' struggle to learn in a classroom setting, all the students, as well as the teacher, must be respectful and encouraging.

CREATING A SAFE AND HOSPITABLE ENVIRONMENT

Henri Nouwen, a spiritual teacher and writer, invites us to look at teaching as a form of hospitality.[11] At the heart of hospitality is the host's commitment to welcoming guests and being present to support and guide them. When the guests are familiar to us, we usually have no trouble welcoming them. However, it may be more difficult to welcome strangers, for strangers often evoke fear in us, and we are quick to become defensive in our interactions with them. Our students are strangers when they arrive in our classrooms and offices. We have probably not met them before and many of them will likely be ethnically, culturally, and racially different from us. The challenge of undertaking teaching as a form of hospitality is to welcome all—not with fear, but with curiosity.

"Who are these people?" I wonder at the beginning of a class. "What do they want? What gifts do they bring?" When we are curious, we have no reason to be defensive. We can welcome these unknown students and wait to see what unfolds.

"In the classroom I want to be a presence to be reckoned with!"

However, being receptive and curious is only half of what defines hospitality. The other half is our willingness to be clear about who we are and what we expect from our students, because a welcoming environment is only possible when we establish clear limits. "When we want to be really hospitable," Nouwen writes, "we not only have to receive strangers but also to meet them by being an unambiguous presence, sharing our ideas, opinions, and lifestyle clearly and distinctly."[12] In the words of a colleague of mine, "In the classroom I want to be a presence to be reckoned with!"

Setting limits is an integral part of hospitality. A space without boundaries is not safe. In my fifth-grade class, boundaries were like a huge rubber fence for the students to bump up against, but not injure themselves in the process. I could post rules or guidelines for behavior, knowing that students would test them to see if they were real. In testing those limits, they discovered more about themselves and more about me, and they could make their own choices on how to behave.

The rule I held to the tightest in those years was that name calling was forbidden. Of course they tested me, referring to others with unkind names within my earshot. When I chastised them, they often defended themselves by saying they were just teasing. I wouldn't argue or try to explain how teasing could be hurtful. I simply repeated that there would be no name calling for any reason in my class.

Of course, some of the students persisted. When it seemed that a particular child was not getting the message, I would angrily confront her, often in front of the class, and remind her, "That behavior is not acceptable." One time, a little girl, in frustration, told me that it didn't really matter because they called each other names on the playground. To this I replied, "I cannot do anything about that but there will be one place in the world where you are safe and that is this classroom." They eventually stopped their mean teasing and if someone slipped up, I would hear another student say, "Hey, shut up! That's not allowed."

In graduate school, I provide students with limits by clearly stating my expectations of them at the beginning of a class. I announce that class will begin on time, with them or without them, and if they are late they will be responsible to find out from another student what they missed. I share with them a little of my experiential teaching style and invite them to participate at whatever level they feel comfortable. I ask them to honor confidentiality. In a more subtle and abstract way I am providing these adults with their own rubber fence!

> "There will be one place in the world where you are safe and that is this classroom."

The importance of a safe and hospitable classroom environment is articulated in the writings of students in a high school English class. Garret Keizer, a teacher, writer, and poet, asked his students to make a journal entry about something "extra" they learned in class—something beyond the lessons provided. Although many responded with their change in attitude toward reading, others wrote about the classroom environment.

"I have learned how a class of students could become more like a family.... We can joke around with each other and have fun but we still get all of our work done," one student wrote. Another explained how a smoothly run classroom, as opposed to a wild one, increases the possibility of learning for everyone. This student learned that in "a good class with manners, respect, and kindness to one another, you learn more and respect the subject matter more."[13]

Providing a safe learning environment in the classroom, workplace, or in an office is easier when the surrounding environment is hospitable, too. Engaging other adults with respect and kindness is an integral part of creating a safe learning environment for teachers as well as students. I believe that this is what makes Kristin Waters so effective as a high school principal. She doesn't expect her teachers to build hospitable classroom environments without experiencing that safety for themselves. Through providing time for teachers to get together for intentional sharing of successes and failures, asking for help, and mentoring one another, the teachers and administrators at South High are building a team. Barbara Stengel, professor of education at Vanderbilt University, says, "Teaching is a team sport. It is not possible, except in the most unusual case, for someone to succeed in a big way on their own. It's too heartbreaking. It's too hard—you need a posse."[14]

ENGAGING KINDLY

Kindness, the ability to be helpful and sympathetic, is considered one of the most influential factors in cultivating healthy, happy adults. A study of twins examined the intelligence and education of the parents, the socioeconomic status of the family, as well as the activities and lessons provided in childhood. None of these mattered as much as having been raised with kindness.[15] Kindness, I believe, is also a foundation of the sacred art of teaching. Whatever we are called to do in our specific teaching situations, we can do it with kindness. We can set limits, correct assignments or behavior, challenge, and discipline kindly. Engaging students kindly can include being strict, demanding, and challenging. Our authority is enhanced rather than undermined by a kind attitude, for students respect teachers who treat them with kindness.

Kindness is shown in a variety of ways. Sometimes it is an encouraging word or a pat on the back. Other times it might be the willingness to listen to students' concerns or take a few moments to inquire about their lives. It might be the way a teacher calls the class to order, how she handles disruptive students, or what he does when faced with a challenge to his authority.

Our individual personality will guide us in how we show kindness. Gilbert Highet, author of *The Art of Teaching*, describes another way of showing kindness by painting a picture of a serious-faced lecturer who rarely calls a student by name but is genuinely interested in making his subject better known and more correctly understood. "If he does not expect all his pupils to grasp its elements at the first attempt but will help the slow and correct the confused, then he will be counted kind, although his face remains immovably grave, and his manner unemotional and impersonal."[16]

> Kindness, I believe, is also a foundation of the sacred art of teaching.... Our authority is enhanced rather than undermined by a kind attitude, for students respect teachers who treat them with kindness.

No matter how we express kindness to our students, we may discover that they are learning to be kind to one another and to us. Kristin Waters told me of a day when she was walking down a busy hallway between classes, frustrated and discouraged. Just to her side came the soft voice of a student, saying respectfully, "You look beautiful today, Miss." His gentle kindness lifted her spirits. Kindness received is as important as kindness offered.

As we discover our own unique ways of sharing kindness with our students, we also need to be willing to treat ourselves kindly. Many teachers judge their performances harshly and feel guilty when they think they haven't done enough for a particular student or class. They spend hours thinking back on a conversation they had with a parent that did not accomplish what they had hoped. They are upset that they lost their temper with one class and can't let go of the bad feelings that generated. We are often much kinder to our students than to ourselves.

Henri Nouwen believes that a possessive sense of responsibility causes a deep sense of inadequacy and self-judgment in many teachers. He advises us to remember that our students are not "ours." They are temporary visitors in our classrooms and our lives, who have been in many rooms before and will be in many rooms after.[17]

When we can gently review a day, a week, or a semester of our teaching with compassion and kindness toward ourselves, we are able to see what we might do differently another time and affirm that we did the best we could, given the situation. Engaging in this practice of kindness toward ourselves, we will be more ready to return to our students with an attitude of hope and possibility. We are not supposed to do this work perfectly, but only to show up with the intention to engage our students with respect and kindness, and create a space where minds and hearts can play.

Looking Inward, Going Deeper

1. Review the nine intelligences discussed on pages 24–27. Which three are your strongest and which are your weakest? Were these ratings true for you when you were a child, a teenager, a young adult? Were you encouraged to explore areas in which you did not excel? To become more aware of the multiple intelligences in your teaching and your life, see if you can pinpoint how others are intelligent.

2. Recall a time you had to struggle to learn something you needed to know. What was it like to persevere? Did you give up? Were you tempted to give up? Did anyone encourage you? Try to rescue you? What did you learn from the experience?

3. Think back to teachers who treated you kindly. What were their various ways of letting you know how they felt about you and other students? What effect did their kindness have on your learning experience? How do you show kindness?

LOVE OF SUBJECT, LOVE OF LEARNING

COMMUNICATING EXCITEMENT AND WONDER

Because I am an expert in my field, I can afford to let go and approach my subject with all the passion of a beginner.

Peter Schneider

Peter Schneider always wanted to be an architect and focused his education to that end. His university program in South Africa was six years, with the fourth year designated for practical experience. He fulfilled that requirement by working with an urban planning and design firm, where he was hired after graduation and eventually became a partner. As one of the top students in his class, he was also offered the opportunity to teach at the university.

Peter found teaching architecture to be far more creative than simply practicing his art. His time at the drawing board was repetitive: designing and redesigning were limited by the expectations of his clients. In the classroom, he felt a freedom to push his students beyond the traditions and conventions of the established architectural community. He subsequently left his practical work for the world of higher education and soon realized he had discovered his vocation.

Peter loves teaching architecture because, along with the skills and information he offers, he guides students into an exploration of their inner lives and the world around them. He is passionate about exploring how the architect's mind, method, and mythologies interact with the natural and cultural landscape. Peter communicates his excitement to his students, often 150 to 250 undergraduates at a time, through his carefully constructed and lively lectures.

Although he has taught the same class for many years, Peter never gives the same lecture twice. He is always uncovering new ideas and surprising insights about himself, his students, and his place in the world. Peter's creativity and his openness to new discoveries are contagious. Guided by intriguing writing assignments, his students explore architecture with both heart and mind.

Peter recognizes that even the youngest undergraduates come to class with at least eighteen years of personal environmental and design experience that can bolster their study of architecture. He requires short written stories about particular moments in their lives, such as a description of some structure they built for themselves when they were children—a secret fort beneath the cellar stairs or a box made into a cave. He asks the students for descriptions of a room they disliked being in and another that made them especially happy. He has them write about a staircase, a doorway, or a front porch they remember. These assignments help students realize how much they already know and how vibrant the world of architecture can be. They also help Peter continue to learn about his students, himself, and architecture itself. "Because I am an expert in my field," he told me, "I can afford to let go and approach my subject with all the passion of a beginner."

THE LEARNER WITHIN

In Chapter 2 we explored the idea of the teacher within every student and within every teacher. We can refer to this teacher within all of us as the inner wisdom that we saw in Lynn's discovery of infinity, as well as in Peter drawing forth the wisdom that comes from the lived experiences of his students. This inner wisdom is the part of ourselves that knows more than we realize.

In the sacred art of teaching, teachers honor and respect that inner wisdom in both their students and themselves. The Sufi tradition admonishes teachers that "there is no credit to them or their students if students sit at their feet forever rather than learning to connect with their own inner teacher."[1] When students do discover their own wisdom, we celebrate if we hear them ask a wise question we have never before considered, offer a new insight expressed in poetic language, or make an interesting connection between disciplines. We recognize that wisdom in ourselves when a new way of explaining a concept comes to mind in the middle of a lesson, or when we find just the right words to confront, and at the same time comfort, a frustrated and resistant student.

While we recognize and affirm our inner teachers—our inner wisdom—I believe we may not pay enough attention to the learner within each of us. We assume that learner is present in our students, for they are in the class to learn. But learning may just be the role they are playing at this time. For all sorts of reasons, their inner learner may have gone to sleep, been wounded by harsh remarks from another teacher, or been discounted by a person in authority. How many of our students have a history of being told they were slow learners or not good at math, ridiculed for asking questions, or made fun of when they responded incorrectly? The inner learner in each of our students may need healing before they can engage the subject matter at any heartfelt level.

Teachers' inner learners must likewise be kept strong and be an integral part of their teaching experience. We are at risk if we begin to feel that there is nothing new to learn about our subject, if we are bored with new information, or if we simply become lazy. One risk is thinking that we know enough to teach a class the way we did before and need not bother to look for new material or creative ways to explain familiar concepts. When our inner learners are alive and well, we can remain excited about our subjects and our teaching becomes lively.

Think for a moment about two people in a classroom or office. One is the teacher and one is the student. Those are the roles they are playing. One teaches, the other learns. There is no variation, no nuance, no subtle exchanges, no spark. They are locked into the roles they have been assigned. However, if we imagine that same scenario recognizing that there are actually four people in that room—the teacher's inner wisdom and inner learner, and the student's inner teacher and inner learner—the possibilities for interaction and engagement multiply exponentially.

Let's suppose a student's inner learner asks a question. If the teacher is living only within his role as authority, he might answer automatically, even if he doesn't really understand the question. But if his inner learner is engaged, he might ask a question to clarify the original question, thereby realizing that the student is onto something new and wants to explore the question more deeply. By witnessing what is happening in the teacher, the student may realize that her question is coming from a deep place within, and therefore has great value in the teaching-learning process. She is no longer just the student; for a moment she has become her teacher's teacher and they are learning together.

I imagine that you have experienced this dynamic in the classroom, or with your children, friends, and colleagues. Something wonderful happens when we realize that, whatever our age or our roles, we are all simultaneously teachers and learners. When that occurs, questions are taken seriously and pondered, not necessarily answered. Ideas are shared and deemed valuable without requiring a relevance to the subject at hand. A classroom may become noisy with excitement, but people listen to one another and everyone's voice is welcome.

> Something wonderful happens when we realize that, whatever our age or our roles, we are all simultaneously teachers and learners.

As teachers, honoring our inner learners in no way discounts what we know or undermines the wonder of sharing our knowledge with our students. We honor what we know, at the same time realizing how much we don't know and how much more there is to learn. Being in touch with this dynamic, even with two hundred students, allows Peter to claim his expertise, even as he acknowledges that in some ways he is still a beginner. When we engage our subject matter and our students as both teacher and learner, we breathe life into our courses and the material we are there to teach.

WHEN THE SUBJECT IS ALIVE

From your years as a student, I imagine you have had teachers who seemed to kill off their subject matter through boredom or lack of excitement. There may have been others who gave the impression that they alone knew the material, so there was nothing new to discover. And hopefully you have had teachers who have made even the driest subject sing.

was the case of my husband's college geology professor. Jim was required to have a science course on his transcript to graduate, and geology seemed to be the easiest way to satisfy that requirement. What he discovered in Dr. McGannon's class was a whole new wonderful world of the earth's materials and processes.

Dr. McGannon was so passionate about geology that his students affectionately nicknamed him "Dr. Rocks." His eyes would shine as he taught them about the different types of rocks, where they could be found, how old they were, and how they were formed. He took his students into the surrounding landscapes to discover for themselves the magic of geology in the middle of their lives. To this day, Jim is fascinated by rocks, collecting them along trails, and sorting and displaying them at home. He often gives a grateful nod to an old professor who breathed life into dry stones.

> Hopefully you have had teachers who have made even the driest subject sing.

Sometimes it is not the subject that excites a teacher, but rather how the subject matter can become a vehicle for something else. This was true for Peter Baer in his English classes. When his inner knowing directed him toward the classroom, he realized he could not teach his first love, philosophy, for very few public secondary schools offer such a course. Although he liked history, he felt he did not know enough to teach that, so he turned to English. Peter is not as excited about English as Dr. Rocks was about geology. But he is passionate about ideas. The liveliness in Peter's teaching comes from the ideas that are inherent in literature—the questions of social justice that stories raise, and the lived experience his students bring to their reading and writing of poetry. Peter's love of ideas is passionate and contagious.

In lower grades, with younger children, the love of subject looks different. Teachers may not be as passionate about
the basics that are required
in preschool, kindergar-   "The world is my classroom
ten, and the early grades,   and life is my subject!"
but they can approach their
teaching with excitement and wonder as they watch children
learn. Ms. Thompson, a first-grade teacher who had been
in the same classroom for thirty-two years, told a school
administrator who was urging her to teach another grade, "I
never tire of teaching children to read," she said. "Each child
learns differently, a variety of methods are necessary, some
struggle, others sail right through, and I get to watch them
open to new and wonderful worlds. Why would I want to
do anything else?"

Jessica Yeager is homeschooling her three children: twin
girls, age five; and a little sister, age two. "The world is my
classroom and life is my subject!" she exclaimed when I asked
her to talk about what and how she teaches. "I take the girls
into the world," she said. "Inside our home, and outside in the
garden, in the neighborhood, to friends' houses. All three are
like sponges, soaking up everything through all five senses.
They ask so many questions, many that I can't answer, so we
search together for the information they want."

Homeschooling allows Jessica to integrate teaching and
learning, excluding nothing. She loves her daughters' spiritual
questions, such as wondering if God lives in the clouds, or
asking why they were born. "In the public schools so much of
life gets separated into compartments," she said. "This subject,
that teacher, homework, recess. I believe life and learning are
all of a piece and I want to experience that with my girls."
The girls are learning to teach each other as Jessica learns
from them and they all learn from exploring the world around

them. When I asked her how long she thought she would homeschool her daughters, she said she didn't know. She is attuned to their interests and desires. She trusts that they will know what they need.

TRUSTING THE LEARNERS' NEEDS

Joey Chernila echoes that trust in the wisdom of even very young children from his own experience at age five. His parents had enrolled him in a preschool close to their home, and he hated it. He told his family he didn't want to go back, he wasn't learning anything, and the children were not being treated kindly. One day, after school, when his mother picked him up and took him to a park to play, Joey climbed to the top of the slide and shouted to his mother, "I am not coming down until you promise you will take me to another school. I will stay here all night if I have to!" Some parents might see that behavior as disobedient, disrespectful, or even a form of blackmail. But Joey's mother was willing to learn from her son's insight into what was right for him. She took him at his word and promised to find him another placement. She discovered a Montessori school not too far away that Joey loved and where he thrived. You will not be surprised to learn that thirty years later Joey is a preschool teacher in a Montessori classroom.

In the Montessori system, like the homeschooling Jessica's daughters are experiencing, learning takes place in line with the children's interests. The Montessori classroom environment is designed for exploration, filled with materials and equipment for learning. Behavior guidelines are established and then the children find their own way from activity to activity. Some might stay with one pursuit for hours; others may move quickly from one task to another. The teacher works like a flame that heats, enlivens, and invites.

Joey told me his most important teaching tool is the clip-board on which he makes notes about what he witnesses. "The hardest thing for me to do is to stay quiet and not interfere," he said. "My personality is generally loud and boisterous, so I have to put the mute button on myself and step back. I am so tempted to encourage or rescue, but if I do, the child learns to turn outside herself rather than find the way within."

Joey and Jessica are both engaged in teaching in what is often called a "learner-centered" classroom or environment. The students set the pace and choose what they need to learn, guided by the teachers. This is the essence of the Montessori system and aspects of the learner-centered model are often integrated into more standard classrooms that use a "teacher-centered" or a "subject-centered" model with students of all ages.

THE CONTINUALLY SHIFTING CENTER

The teacher-centered model has fallen out of favor at all levels of education in the last twenty or twenty-five years. It calls forth the image of an expert lecturing his or her students, who are assumed to be beginners with nothing to bring to the learning process. Parker J. Palmer names the pupils in this situation amateurs:

> People without training and full of bias, who depend on the experts for objective or pure knowledge. This objective knowledge flows downstream with no chance of subjectivity flowing back up.[2]

As I thought about my own teaching and learning experiences, I recognized that this is not how I teach. I find it impossible to lecture for more than twenty minutes. I depend on student involvement to keep my teaching lively. Yet I believe the teacher-centered approach may be the right model for some teachers, students, and subject matter. What comes to mind is my attempt to learn biblical Hebrew.

When I went into the class I knew nothing about the language. I had no familiarity with the alphabet, hadn't realized that the writing went right to left, and was totally confused by the pronunciation. I was a complete amateur. I needed everything the professor knew and sent downstream. There was no way I could respond effectively; I simply had to receive and take in as much as I could, which wasn't a lot. There was little interaction between teacher and student or among the students. The one time we were asked to hold a conversation with a classmate, I was paired with a young woman who had lived in Israel for a year and was familiar with modern Hebrew. She kept telling me how easy it was to learn this language!

Sometimes a professor might begin with this teacher-centered method and then gradually let go of the one-way flow and begin to recognize the value of the students' lived experience. Remember Dana Wilbanks, who started his graduate school teaching in a totally teacher-centered way—in love with his subject matter, spending hours creating lectures for his students, teaching as he had been taught throughout his schooling? He soon realized that this was not the only way and, with the help of his colleagues, he discovered how to become a more subject-centered teacher.

In the subject-centered classroom, the image of objective knowledge flowing downstream turns into an image of a circle with the subject matter at the center. All the learners—teacher and students alike—gather around the subject. Everyone has access to the subject and to each other. This interaction among the learners about the subject reflects "complex patterns of communication—sharing observations and interpretations, correcting and complementing each other, torn by conflict in this moment and joined by consensus in the next."[3]

Have you experienced a classroom that is designed this way, either as a teacher or as a learner? I believe my teaching about prayer, whether in the academic classroom, in churches, or on retreat is subject-centered. I place prayer at the center of the circle and through a variety of activities we dance around it, agreeing, disagreeing, sharing information, responding, remembering personal experiences, and asking questions of one another. I do not hold back the knowledge I possess from my many years of studying prayer, but that knowledge is simply part of the subject to be observed and interpreted by all of us together.

In a conversation with a young man about his experiences in high school, he told me of the eye-opening experience he had in American history. The teacher presented information, facts, figures, and dates to be learned, but she was not the center of the class. The focus of attention—the real subject— was always the idea that the study of history could inform the students about their own lives and have bearing on the future. Each historical event was presented to be examined, explored, and questioned. Students were introduced to the idea that history written from one perspective was never the full picture. "We were asked to consider other possible perspectives," he told me excitedly. "She would ask us to think about what the history of the Civil War might look like through the eyes of slaves, or how women's stories change the image of the industrial revolution." In this subject-centered classroom the teacher encouraged her students to look beyond the facts to discover for themselves new possibilities in the study of history.

I don't believe that any classroom is purely teacher-centered, subject-centered, or learner-centered. Steve Replogle's fourth-grade class is teacher-centered in the first few weeks of school. As the year progresses and he deems the students ready, he begins to gradually release his responsibility, encouraging his students to take responsibility for more of their own learning.

Joey Chernila admits that while the Montessori philosophy calls for student-centered learning, there are times when the classroom must become teacher-centered. The teacher creates an environment for active learning that includes not only a wide variety of learning possibilities, but respect and kindness as well. Students need to be taught guidelines for their behavior, so as they go about their own learning, they are not interfering with the activities of another child.

In my own prayer classes, I have let go of the subject-centered model to lecture on the Christian mystics, recognizing that the students need to be introduced to these important people in the Christian tradition. Most of the students know little about these historical figures. They are beginners, or amateurs, and they need some basic knowledge about the social, religious, and political times in which the mystics lived.

In th[e] subject-centered classroom the teacher encourage[s] her students to look beyond the facts to discover for themselves new possibilities.

For a few class periods the information simply flows downstream. After the lectures, the mystics themselves become the subject at the center of the class. Students are then encouraged to delve more deeply into the lives of different mystics and to ponder how these medieval and contemporary figures have influenced their religious traditions and their own personal prayer lives.

This shifting center from one teaching situation to another creates a lively classroom. However, one of the difficulties for all teachers is when we prefer subject-centered teaching and the students we have that year, or in one particular class, are not ready to share responsibility or able to direct their own learning.

In elementary schools, if you wish to explore subject-centered learning and the students' previous teacher used a strict teacher-centered approach, you will have students who only experience themselves as amateurs and believe that all they have to do is listen to the teacher impart knowledge. When this happens, much time and energy needs to be spent carefully drawing out their inner wisdom before they are ready to take on some of the responsibility for their own progress. There will be a certain amount of chaos and confusion as this happens, and you may be judged harshly for not having good classroom management. But by being willing to expose students of any age to a variety of teaching and learning methods, you are instilling in your students a love of learning that will last a lifetime.

LIFELONG LEARNING

When we embrace lifelong learning and become learner-centered teachers,[4] we experience teaching as a sacred art. Learner-centered teachers are excited by learning, not only in their own fields but also in areas outside their expertise. They model for their students the possibility of remaining curious about the world, open to new ideas, and being willing to pursue new interests for no reason at all except for the love of learning.

Gilbert Highet defines the ideal teacher as one with "exceptionally wide and lively intellectual interests such as an active enthusiasm for the problems of the mind, an inexhaustible pleasure of the arts, and who spends the whole of his or her life widening the horizons of the spirit."[5] Quite a tall order! But if you look at the teachers you remember, I imagine that through their teaching and sharing in the classroom or seminar you knew they were lifelong learners. Maybe they told stories about an Outward Bound adventure they took one summer, how hard it is to be learning the guitar at fifty-five, or what they discovered about the universe when they had the opportunity to look through a high-powered telescope.

As lifelong learners, we need to remember that teaching, as well as originating as sacred calling, is a craft that can and must be learned. Our passion for teaching does not automatically prepare us for the classroom, the workplace, or the tutoring we might be doing. Many of us arrive at our new schools woefully unprepared for the realities of the classroom. In those first years, we need to learn from more experienced teachers, not just the theories of education but also ways to handle the nitty-gritty situations we encounter. We also need to be willing to learn from our mistakes. Like mastering any subject or skill, learning to teach takes time and practice.

Our students know we are lifelong learners when we are willing to try new teaching methods, and to be open to a student who challenges our assumptions or points out that we were misinformed or that we made a mistake. This happened to me years ago when I was teaching continuing education classes for teachers. I told a story about my family of origin in which I called one of my uncles the black sheep of his generation. I thought nothing of it until, after class, one of my African-American students took me aside and said gently, "That was a racist statement you made this morning." I searched my memory and looked bewildered until she said, "Black sheep." I had been completely unaware of the undercurrents of racism inherent in that familiar phrase. I apologized profusely, and she kindly said, "No need to go on and on. I simply respect you too much to not let you know that what you said was offensive."

I had another cultural learning experience from a Korean student in a doctoral program I was facilitating. One of the other students asked me how I should be addressed, with what title, and I responded, "Please, just call me Jane." The young Korean man was horrified. "Oh, no," he said, "I could never do that. In my culture it would be most impolite and not allowed." Because I wanted this small seminar to be informal, I didn't want to be called Professor or Reverend Vennard, so he and I finally decided on Reverend Jane. Using my first name still made him a little uncomfortable, but the title before it made it possible for him to honor his culture as well as my desire for informality.

Recognizing the opportunity for learning in any situation distinguishes lifelong learning from what is often called continuing education. Columbia Theological Seminary drew attention to this difference when the school renamed its continuing education program and building the Center for Lifelong Learning. Seminary leaders did this because of their desire to recognize that *continuing education* usually implies that we need someone else to teach us, and that we enroll in a program to get a degree or a certificate—something to indicate we have advanced in our careers. By contrast, *lifelong learning* speaks of the never-ending process of the development of mind, heart, and spirit. As theology professor Wayne Whitson Floyd writes, "Continuing education leads us *to know* something different; lifelong learning assumes that we will *be* someone different as a result of the process."[6]

Teaching is a sacred art precisely because we recognize the transformative power of the teaching-learning process. We are not simply imparting information that we hope our students will receive, but are also involved in the process of shaping our own and our students' lives. The information and the subjects we teach are important, for they are the vehicles through which this takes place. Think of the light in a student's eyes when she has an insight that will forever change her view of the world, or when he asks a question that is at the core of the issue and he recognizes the wonder of his own mind. These are transformative moments for the students—and for us—as we realize that our vocation, the hard day-to-day work of teaching, can contribute to the unfolding and flowering of the students who have been entrusted to our care.

> Teaching is a sacred art precisely because we recognize the transformative power of the teaching-learning process.

Looking Inward, Going Deeper

1. Have you had teachers who loved their subjects? What was it like to learn from them? What do you love about your subject and what do you love about teaching it?

2. What are your experiences, as both teacher and student, of teacher-centered, subject-centered, or learner-centered classroom methods?

3. How alive is your inner learner? Think back on a time when a student taught you something new. What was that like?

4. How do you feel about keeping up with new developments in your field? When was the last time you explored a new area of learning?

CHAPTER FOUR

USING SACRED LANGUAGE

TELLING STORIES, ASKING QUESTIONS, AND LISTENING WELL

I made a mistake last week. I'm sorry.

Holly Heuer

The students in the second week of their three-hour preaching seminar were upset. They had been excited the week before when they met their professor, Reverend Holly Heuer. She was a pastor in a local church with many years of preaching experience and was bright and funny and very knowledgeable. As she outlined the material they would cover and her expectations of the class, they knew they were embarking on a unique experience in their seminary education.

The next week, Holly brought a visitor to class. He was a colleague who was interested in her teaching assignment, and she invited him to join them for a few weeks so he could see what they were doing. The students were uncomfortable with the subtle changes brought about by this new person in their midst. They had just begun to form a community and

here was a stranger whose interactions with them were dis-
orienting, confusing, and distracting. That evening there was
buzz on social media, with the students telling each other how
disappointed they were about this change in class and email-
ing Holly to ask for an explanation of the man's presence. It
became quite clear that they did not want the class to be open
to visitors.

Holly told me later how upset she had been with this
outpouring of feelings. She was teaching the class for the first
time and, along with her excitement, she was nervous about
how effective she would be. As the third class approached, she
had worked herself into major anxiety and wondered if she
would be able to go back. In desperation she called a friend to
help her sort it out.

"That conversation was a lifesaver," she told me later.
"As I poured out my story to my friend, she listened to the
whole thing, and then she paused and said to me gently,
'Holly, you made a mistake.' With that response the anxiety
dropped away. I was creating a disaster out of a simple mistake." Holly then called the visiting colleague and told him
frankly that she had changed her mind and she was rescind-
ing her invitation.

The next class began with silent tension as the students
waited to see what would happen. Holly took a deep breath
and then said, "I made a mistake last week. I shouldn't have
invited him. I'm sorry." One student said later, "It was like
the breath being held by everyone in the room was let go in a
huge collective sigh. The amazing thing was that Holly said
no more about it. She didn't explain or defend her action.
She just smiled, clearly feeling the relief herself, and began
class with a discussion of the reading assignment. We knew
in that moment that she spoke from her heart and could be
trusted."

The Languages We Use

Eugene Peterson, author and biblical scholar, wrote in *The Contemplative Pastor* about the three languages prevalent in our culture: informational, motivational, and personal.[1] All are necessary in the teaching-learning process, but he highlights the importance of personal language.

Informational language consists of facts and data now electronically available at our fingertips. Gone are the series of encyclopedias, thick dictionaries, and cumbersome card catalogs in the library. If you want to know something, a few clicks on the computer will bring you the information you need.

Informational language is the foundation for most teaching. We are responsible for offering our students facts relevant to our subject matter. Young children need to know the alphabet, names for objects, and how to count. Children love information and are excited about how much they know. When my stepson Jamie was ten, he told me excitedly that he knew the phone numbers of all his friends and proceeded to tell me all twenty-eight of them!

As students grow older they learn new vocabulary, become familiar with basic historical information, and are offered scientific facts. Students feel competent as they acquire new information and can name all the state capitals, recite a poem, or explain to you how the body's digestive system works. If you are a teacher in a specific subject area at any level of education, you most likely have a wealth of information about your specialty and enjoy sharing it with your students. You may even be an expert in your field.

However, if you use only informational language, your students will soon tune you out. Information by itself is dry and unappealing. How long can you listen to a lecture that is strictly informational? Even if I am interested in the subject,

I have about a ten-minute attention span. In a more informal setting, think of the times someone who has a passion about a certain topic corners you and goes on and on, regaling you with facts. When that happens to me, I may politely smile and nod, but my mind and heart are far away. I might have become engaged if I had been given some reason to care about the many facts being offered.

Peterson calls the second language "motivational." This language is used to convince the hearer of something. It is used in conjunction with informational language and can be seen most readily in advertising and political campaigns. Information about the product or the candidate is projected in such a way that you are motivated to buy what is being sold or to vote for a particular candidate.

In teaching, motivational language is more subtle than informational language, and is often communicated through tone of voice, attitude, and example. Remember "Dr. Rocks," whose passion for geology was the motivating factor in his teaching? He didn't spend much time telling his students why they should love geology or how important it was to learn about rocks. He didn't use many words to motivate his students. Living and teaching his passion comprised all the motivational language he needed. If he had only used words to try to convince his students to engage with the information, I imagine that would have backfired. Wordy explanations of why our students should love the content of our teaching don't usually work. They are growing up in a culture that is continually trying to convince them of something—what to buy, how to act, whom to vote for, and what to think. Our students have a healthy distrust of overt motivational language. They want something more.

Personal language is Peterson's third category. Using personal language brings the hearts of both teacher and learner into the conversation. Informational and motivational languages are not ignored; rather, personal language takes the facts to a deeper level. Personal language from both teachers and learners helps them step out from behind their roles and become real to one another.

EXPLORING THE POWER OF PERSONAL LANGUAGE

In the story at the beginning of this chapter, Holly was using personal language when she spoke honestly from her heart: "I made a mistake." She didn't give any additional information about her guest, or her process of working through her confusion. She didn't ask for or try to motivate her students to understand or forgive her. Her simple statement was enough and provides an example of what Episcopal

> Our students have a healthy distrust of overt motivational language. They want something more.

priest and college professor Barbara Brown Taylor believes: "In a word-clogged world, the only words that stand a chance of getting people's attention are simple, honest words that come from everyday life."[2]

A number of years ago, I gave a presentation stripped of all personal language. A friend, who was a Catholic priest, asked me to teach an afternoon workshop for the teachers of a Catholic school. I was excited by the opportunity and we planned together the best way to approach this particular group of teachers. With our planning complete, I asked him if he thought that the teachers would mind that I wasn't Catholic. He replied offhandedly, "You don't need to tell them."

I decided to follow his advice and I went to this workshop determined to hide my Protestant roots. What a terrible and exhausting experience. Throughout the presentations, the exercises we had designed, and my interactions with the participants, I told no stories and was constantly monitoring myself so as not to reveal my true identity. In one of the evaluations of the afternoon one person wrote, "The material was interesting and valuable, but the presenter seemed cold and detached."

At the heart of personal language is the pronoun *I*. Using the word *I* lets learners know there is a real person sharing information with them. If students make statements with which you disagree, you might say, "I think there are other ways of understanding this," rather than telling them, "You're wrong." I-statements leave room for connection and conversation, whereas pronouncements raise defenses and lead to closed minds and hearts. Wouldn't you prefer that someone say, "I believe," to open a conversation, rather than assigning the belief statement to an unknown source, such as "Everyone believes," or "It is believed"?

> At the heart of personal language is the pronoun *I*.

Personal language does not take the place of motivational language and information, or substitute opinion for fact. Instead, it weaves the teacher into the content. A teacher may tell stories based on lived experience, such as letting students know how hard it was for him to learn geometry, or how the book being studied had deeply influenced a major decision in her life. As you look back at your own learning, I imagine you can remember a personal story a teacher told you, either in class or in a private conversation. I also imagine many of you have been integrating stories naturally and easily in your own teaching for years.

I often hear teachers wondering how much personal information is appropriate in the teaching-learning process. Self-revelation can be misused. If teachers are looking for sympathy, affirmation, or understanding, they are using the classroom or the students to fulfill their own needs. When deciding whether to include a story in my teaching, I ask myself if the story is going to enhance the student's learning or whether the story is just about me. Sometimes it is hard to tell the difference, and I have often made mistakes. But I remain watchful by reevaluating my motivation for the storytelling after the fact.

In addition to personal stories, information comes alive with anecdotes about the scientist who made a great discovery or stories about the personal lives of historical figures. In a literature class in college, my professor always told some story about the life of the author whose work we were reading. Along with holding our interest, these anecdotes provided context for our studies. Her method made such a deep impression on me that all these years later I still seek out stories about authors when I am having trouble understanding their words.

As we use more personal language with our students, we can also invite them to use personal language in response to the content we are teaching. That was what architecture professor Peter Schneider was doing when he asked students to write about their lived experience with buildings, rooms, porches, or doorways. Although those assignments were written for him, I can imagine in a smaller group that the students could share their experiences with each other. In spiritual formation workshops, I often ask participants to reflect on a personal experience and then share their reflection with one or two other people. These stories are not for me, but rather are designed for people to make connections with each other and the material as they share and listen. The combination of personal sharing and deep listening creates the conditions for the conversation to lead to dialogue.

RECOGNIZING THE DIFFERENCES BETWEEN DIALOGUE AND DEBATE

Dialogue is the opposite of debate. Debate uses mostly informational language and is like a contest in which there are winners and losers. In debate we listen to others to discover what is missing from or flawed in their argument. As we listen, we make note of those flaws and prepare ourselves to expose them in order to prove the other person wrong and to poke holes in the opponent's overall position. Although we are familiar with formal debates in our political life, they abound in all sorts of other places and situations.

Imagine a meeting called by the school principal to discuss a new reading curriculum. Although it may be called a discussion, it often is little more than a polite debate. Teachers may come with their minds made up, prepared to argue for what they believe to be the best way to teach reading. They then listen to one another with the sole purpose of looking for the opportunity of presenting their information about why they think one system is better than another. Everyone is talking, or planning to talk. No one is really listening.

Different issues but similar debates erupt spontaneously in classrooms all the time. How quickly a discussion can turn into an argument! The issue might be about what game to play at recess or the planning of a middle school field trip. Debates on social issues, religious beliefs, or ethical behavior catch fire in high schools and colleges.

To shift a group from debate to dialogue cannot be done in the heat of the moment, unless those involved have some information and understanding about the two ways of communicating. For this reason, I think it is wise to specifically teach the differences between them before debating gets into full swing. One way to explain the difference is that dialogue has an entirely different intention from debate. Rather than listening to gather ammunition to defeat the other person, in dialogue we listen for understanding, for what might be insightful and true in the other's experience. We are seeking common ground.

Another aspect of dialogue that needs to be articulated is that silence is an integral part of the conversation, as well as clarifying questions and expressions of appreciation for what has been offered. In a dialogue someone might say in response to your idea, "How interesting. I've never looked at it that way." Wouldn't those words make you feel respected? Another response that promotes dialogue might be, "I'm not sure I understand. Could you help me out?"

When students are familiar with the terminology and have experienced the difference in calmer moments, a reminder to the class could change the conversation. "Let's shift this from a debate to a dialogue" might be enough. Or "Stop! No one is listening to anyone else" speaks to the need for different behaviors. Teaching about dialogue is an ongoing process and none of us ever becomes an expert. But it is a skill that can be learned and practiced in a variety of situations.

The hardest part of engaging in dialogue with others is that all participants must be willing for their minds and hearts to be changed. I admit that I am not always willing to be that open, and I am sure many students are not willing or able to engage at that level. Dialogue takes time and energy and has to be done in a trusting environment. Not all situations in schools and communities are safe and respectful. Even when I want to be part of a dialogue instead of a debate, and I begin to feel I am not being heard, I can easily slide into debate mode, get judgmental and frustrated, and make the situation worse.

Whatever our prior experience with debate and dialogue, we can offer guidelines and entertain the possibility of dialogue. Let's go back to that hypothetical faculty meeting to discuss the new reading curriculum. If those in attendance engage in dialogue rather than debate, there would be more personal language used. Teachers could talk about their experience with different curriculums. One parent might share how his child had benefited from one program and another how her child had learned through a different method. Everyone doesn't have to agree, but experiences and ideas are listened to and treated with respect. Everyone listens for ideas they might find useful. They listen carefully, sorting though their own biases, to make room for a solution that contains a little bit of everyone's truth. For this to happen, participants need to listen deeply to one another.

> "My own experiences as a student have shown me the importance of a teacher who listens well."

LEARNING TO LISTEN, HONORING SILENCE

Bryan McCord, a student at the Iliff School of Theology, wrote a reflection paper about the skills he would need to become an authentic teacher:

> If I cannot listen well to a student in the class or be seen as approachable for advice or questions after a class—regardless of who or what I am teaching—then I would consider my educational wherewithal to be lacking. My own experiences as a student have shown me the importance of a teacher who listens well, furthering my realization that this is a powerful and challenging skill, neither to be taken for granted nor neglected in the classroom setting.

Early in my teaching career I learned the technique of active listening. We were taught to reflect back what we heard to the person who was speaking—not only the words spoken but also the feelings behind them. I had my doubts, but one day on playground duty a little second grader came running up to me, shouting and weeping, "He stole my ball! He stole my ball!" Taking a deep breath, I replied, "Wow! That is really making you angry!" "Yeah!" he said over his shoulder as he ran back to the game. I was amazed. Before learning this technique, I would have taken his hand and gone with him to solve the problem. I realized he didn't need help—he needed to be heard.

As useful as active listening was on the playground, a colleague pointed out to me some problems inherent in the technique. Kindergarten teacher Kimberly Browne worked for a principal one year who used this technique with his teachers. She would go to him with a problem she needed help with or to discuss something she thought had to be changed. He would always reply with "You sound confused," or "I hear your concern." He would never respond with anything substantial based on his own opinion or experience. "It made me so mad," she told me. "I wanted him to talk to me, argue with me, confront me." When she told him that was what she wanted from him he said, "You sound disappointed." If she shouted her feelings, he would respond, "Wow, are you angry!" Kimberly said it was like talking to a balloon—everything just bounced back. There was no engagement.

The true and deep listening that Bryan wants to bring to his teaching is not a technique but an orientation of heart that makes one vulnerable. "To truly listen," says Native American elder Sa'k'ej Hendersong, "is to risk being changed forever."[3] To listen deeply to another we must be willing to be silent, for only in the silence can we actually hear and feel what is being said and then have time to reflect before we respond. Learning to listen well calls us to the practice of silence in the midst of conversation.

Common conversational patterns in our culture include talking over one another, finishing each other's sentences, interrupting a story with a story of our own, asking unnecessary questions, or offering advice. We listen only with one ear while we formulate words for the next opportunity to break in. One way to practice silence is to become aware of our own conversational patterns, choose to be silent, and allow the speaker to finish his or her thought. In this way we give our full attention to what is being said. We can let the other know we are listening though our body language and murmurs. Or we might say, when a response is required, "Let me think about that for a moment," or ask a question, such as "Could you tell me more about that?" This kind of open-ended question is an important part of sacred language and lets students know they are respected and heard.

Expanding Our Use of Questions and Answers

A basic rhythm in the teaching-learning process is for the teacher to offer information and then, after a suitable length of time, ask the students questions to see if they respond with the right answers. Think of elementary school teachers calling out multiplication questions and the whole class responding with the answers, or giving a spelling or vocabulary test where there was only one right answer to each question. Throughout school, multiple-choice tests are given to assess progress. Even in tests with essay questions, the answers will usually be judged according to what the instructor believes to be correct. These methods are effective in determining how much factual material the student is grasping and will remain part of classroom landscapes. But with our exploration of personal language and dialogue, we might be able to expand our use of questions and answers.

Remember the story of Lynn in her math class? The teacher asked the students, "What is zero divided by one?" and the whole class shouted, "zero!" Then he asked: "What is one divided by zero?" and again the class shouted "zero!" The teacher paused to ask if everyone agreed, and he waited to see if anyone would come up with a different answer. His silence gave Lynn the time to formulate her own answer, find her inner wisdom, and respond. The teacher's silence in that process was the key.

> The teacher's silence in [the learning] process [i]s the key.

In the fifth-grade class I was teaching, I became aware that when I asked a general question of the students, hands would immediately shoot up, indicating the desire to answer. And these hands always belonged to the same students. I would wait for a moment to see if any other hands were raised, and when none appeared, I would call on one of those whose hands had been waving. It occurred to me that all those waving hands discouraged some of my students who needed more time to reflect on the question. I introduced a timer to the class, and when I asked a question, students were not allowed to raise their hands until the buzzer went off. This slowed down the process and gave all students an opportunity to struggle with the question and think more deeply about it. Speed was no longer rewarded. Many more students began to respond to the questions and more voices were heard.

In addition to integrating silence into our questioning, it is wise to begin to include in our teaching questions that have no right answer. Novelist Marilynne Robinson responded in an interview about her experience of teaching: "We have created a culture of 'right' answers. You can actually freeze people, even in their own thoughts, by giving them conclusions."[4] Many questions do have right and wrong answers, while other questions involve ideas, opinions, and flights of fancy. Such questions prompt students to respond creatively and in personal language. These questions can be called "honest, open questions," a term that comes from the Quaker tradition.

Part of that religious tradition is a process called the "clearness committee." When people in the community are trying to make an important decision, they gather a group of six or eight people to spend a few hours with them. The guidelines are simple. The one who has called the meeting, often referred to as the focus person or the storyteller, states as clearly as possible the issue that needs resolution—including background, pertinent facts, feelings, and the confusion he may be experiencing. The committee then sits in silence until honest, open questions arise from the hearts of the listeners. These questions are defined as hav-

"You can actually freeze people, even in their own thoughts, by giving them conclusions."

ing no "yes" or "no" answer, for those single-word answers put an abrupt stop to deeper reflection. "Have you talked to your parents about this?" is not an honest, open question, whereas "If you talked to your parents about this, how do you imagine they might respond?" encourages the focus person to think more broadly.

Another sign of an honest, open question is that the questioner has no idea how the person will respond. "How might this issue relate to an earlier experience in your life?" would be honest and open. A less logical and more surprising question might be, "What color is your dilemma?" Honest, open questions are not based on unspoken assumptions, nor do they try to lead the storyteller in any particular direction. "I hear anger in your voice. How is that related to your issue?" assumes the storyteller is angry and guides her to explore her anger. "What feelings are you experiencing right now in the telling of this story?" is honest and open.

When the environment is safe and deeply respectful, the questioners have the opportunity to learn as much about themselves as the storyteller learns about his response to his dilemma. Committee members often report they might hear a question asked by another member and consider its relevance to their own lives. Or they recognize that a response of the focus person sheds light on a hidden issue of their own.

You may never be called upon to serve on a clearness committee or call one for yourself. But the gift we can receive from the process lies in learning how to ask questions that invite learners to go more deeply into themselves to find their own inner wisdom. However, it is wise to remember that honest, open questions may not be welcome by everyone. Children and teens often block the process with one- or two-word answers, such as "Nothing," in response to "What did you do in school?" or "She's cool" in response to "What do you think about your new teacher?"

Many students are more likely to respond to open-ended questions when they are given assignments that pique their imaginations. As a creative writing assignment, you might suggest that students place themselves as a character in a novel, as an observer in the laboratory of a famous scientist, or as an assistant in an artist's studio, and then ask them to describe what they see and feel. Asking students to choose one phrase or word from a poem that feels particularly powerful to them and have them tell you why is another way to stimulate the use of personal language and creativity.

Questions that invite the imagination are honest and open, such as "Imagine what happens next," "Imagine if you were the brother or sister of that particular person in history," or "Imagine how you would feel if your experiment failed over and over again."

Another opportunity to ask honest, open questions in teaching and learning might be in individual conversations with students, or possibly in parent conferences. In addition to telling the student or parent what you have observed about the student's behavior, abilities, strengths, and weaknesses, ask questions with no preconceived idea of the response, such as "What do you imagine underlies this tendency to avoid tackling a difficult subject?" The answers you receive may help you understand the behaviors you have been observing.

Young people, as well as adults, may experience honest, open questions as invasive. They may not be comfortable with personal language or trust you enough to respond. That can be frustrating if you are hoping for dialogue and it doesn't seem to be forthcoming. Remember that by engaging in this kind of exchange, you make yourself and the other person vulnerable and open to the possibility of being changed. Not everyone is willing to open themselves to that degree.

As we reflect on the questions we ask our students, we might also pay attention to how we encourage students to ask us questions and how we respectfully listen and respond. I had a physics teacher in college who would periodically stop and ask us if we had any questions. She would wait no more than ten seconds and say briskly, "Good. Let's go on." I remember thinking how I didn't know enough to ask a question and the only thing I could think to say was, "Would you please start over?"

When we close off questioning, or respond too quickly, we are probably not listening carefully or taking the question seriously. Sometimes it is wise for us to ask for clarification so we are certain about what is being asked. When I was nine I asked my mother if something I had been taught in Sunday school was true. She asked me to tell her what I had heard and then proceeded to answer me: "Some people think that's true, others don't; you will have to decide for yourself." I was not happy with the answer. I wanted a yes or a no. But

> Rather than offering easy answers that provide temporary safety certainty students need to be encouraged to struggle with the search.

looking back on that conversation I don't believe my mother was avoiding an answer; I think she was letting me know that some questions have no right or wrong answers and that I would have to think for myself and search for understanding.

LIVING THE QUESTIONS

We all want answers to life's perplexing questions. Oftentimes, we want them quickly and to be issued with great conviction. As teachers, we may be tempted to offer these answers instead of helping our students realize that some questions have no absolute answers. Rather than offering easy answers that provide temporary certainty, students need to be encouraged to struggle with the search.

A friend and colleague of mine received a letter from a woman whom he had mentored along her spiritual journey. She wrote of the gift of being allowed to continue her search for a spiritual home and not be given easy answers.

> I can only imagine the narrowness of my life had I followed the urge to be certain, to cozy up with this or that zendo or church and proclaim the angst of searching to be over. I have rarely met a teacher who encouraged me to ask questions, especially about the zendo or the church's definition of itself. You were one of the few who helped

me have the courage to keep asking. In a sense, it's one of the most precious gifts I've ever received.

This woman's experience and her words speak to the lived experience of poet Rainer Maria Rilke's well-known advice to a young poet: "Be patient toward all that is unsolved in your heart and try to love the questions them-

"You were one of the few who helped me have the courage to keep asking."

selves. Live the questions now. Perhaps you will then gradually, without noticing it, live along some distant day into the answer."[5]

Looking Inward, Going Deeper

1. When in your teaching have you experienced the power of using personal language?

2. How do you feel when you get caught in a debate with another person? Do you love the challenge? Do you want to flee? Why do you react this way?

3. When are you apt to cause conversations to turn into debates? Is debate a comfortable communication style for you?

4. A colleague said of a friend, "When he listens I hear what I say." Have you had such an experience of deep listening? What happened as a result of that experience?

5. When in your teaching would the use of honest, open questions in any form be beneficial?

CHAPTER FIVE

CLAIMING OUR AUTHORITY BY LETTING GO OF CONTROL

My authority comes from being trustworthy.

Steve Replogle

Steve is very clear that his authority in the classroom does not derive from his assigned role as teacher. As a beginning teacher, he had assumed that he would be able to control his students' behavior simply because he was the teacher and they were the learners. He quickly discovered that

> "It is the nature of young people to test authority."

wasn't true. "Authority comes from within," he told me. "It comes from my knowing myself and offering who I am to my students."

Steve believes he has earned this authority by being a good instructor and having a healthy relationship with his students. They know that he is teaching them what he loves and in the process he treats his students with love. Steve keeps his promises and the students know that he is trustworthy.

They know this because they have tested him. "It is the nature of young people to test authority," he said, smiling. "I see it as healthy. Anyone can say, 'You can trust me' and then not behave that way. Children are right to watch my actions and not simply believe my words. This way they can know for themselves whether or not I am to be trusted."

Steve follows a regular routine every school day that feels to him like a daily spiritual practice. He goes to school to prepare for the day long before the children arrive. This preparation is not just lesson planning and ordering materials, but also preparing his heart. He likes to think of the individual students who will be entering the room and to anticipate their arrival with curiosity and hope. As they burst through the door, he is there to welcome them as the lively, exciting, frustrating process of teaching and learning begins.

At home in the evening Steve spends time reviewing his day. Not only does he think about the children and what he noticed about their behaviors and attitudes, but he also reflects on his own actions. He remembers the lively moments when the whole class started laughing and almost couldn't stop.

Through his attentiveness to his students and himself, Steve is claiming his authority.

He feels good about how an experimental lesson went, and relishes the creativity that was coming out in the children's writing. Steve also pays attention to the times he got impatient, ignored a student who needed attention, or did not listen well. He does not judge himself: he just notices who he was that day. He may then take that information into prayer, letting go of disappointments and strengthening himself for yet another day. Through his attentiveness to his students and himself, Steve is claiming his authority.

Steve's ritual is not for everyone. Part of experiencing teaching as a sacred art is finding your own way to remain attentive both to your students and to yourself. Some teachers take a walk before school begins to ground themselves in nature and reflect on the day ahead. Others might use their commute time on the way to school for planning and their trip home for reflection. Whether you are in a classroom or another teaching situation that does not involve a group of students, I imagine you have a ritual to prepare yourself for the teaching-learning interaction that helps you claim your authority, even if you were not aware that that was what you were doing.

EXAMINING THE DIFFERENCES BETWEEN AUTHORITY AND POWER

Although a common synonym for *authority* is *power*, I think in our culture we experience the words quite differently. If Steve talked about claiming his power in the classroom, wouldn't you have a different feeling about his pronouncement? This difference may be because we tend to associate power with a hierarchical model, where people in power are placed over and above others. When this happens in extreme situations, those at the bottom are rendered powerless. Teachers may presume that their position gives them power and control over their students. If we enter the classroom expecting this to be true, we are in for a shock. It doesn't take long for us to realize that no matter how much power we think we have, we are not in control.

I remember my fourth-grade teacher who tried so hard to control us. The more she commanded, demanded, threatened, and punished, the worse we got. I think we realized that she wanted us to be powerless and we weren't about to go along with that. It was a very difficult year for all of us.

When school started the next year, our fifth-grade teacher, Mrs. Rust, welcomed us and said sternly, "You children have a bad reputation! I want you to know that your behavior of last year will not be tolerated in my classroom." She paused and looked directly into our eyes. Then she said, "Now, let's get on with the important work of teaching and learning." Mrs. Rust was in charge! What a relief! Students do not like an out-of-control classroom any more than teachers do. But when teachers and students get locked it a pattern of fighting for power, there is often no way out. They are stuck in that struggle as long as they are together.

Mrs. Rust claimed her authority, not to control us, but to establish an environment of respect and caring that was conducive to learning. Spiritual writer Henri Nouwen wrote that "compassionate authority empowers, encourages, calls forth hidden gifts, and enables great thing to happen."[1] Mrs. Rust was a model of compassionate authority. Through her honesty and clarity, her high expectations, and her gentle humor, she guided us in both our behavior and our learning. She was so successful in transforming her unruly group of students that she was promoted with us to sixth grade! We received another blessed year in the presence of that remarkable woman.

SHARING RESPONSIBILITY FOR TEACHING AND LEARNING

In Mrs. Rust's class, guided by her respect and trust for us, we began to assume more and more responsibility for our own learning. This is also the hallmark of Steve's authority, which encourages students in his class to take responsibility for both teaching and learning. Steve, first introduced in Chapter 1, started the year as what I would describe as a teacher-centered instructor, but he moved quickly into what he calls "the gradual release of responsibility." This letting go makes shared responsibility possible.

People behave responsibly when they act on their own initiative and are willing to be accountable for the results of their actions. A responsible student will come up with an idea for a class project and follow it through to completion. Sometimes responsibility is shown when students offer a new idea or request a change of routine for the process of teaching and learning. A graduate student might suggest that the desks be put in a circle to encourage more interaction. An employee might ask that the required meeting be scheduled at noon, rather than after work. A young child might take the chalk from the instructor's hand and say, "I'll do it myself."

We all grow in responsibility by expressing our initiative and becoming more independent. Imagine a line with independent and responsible adults at one end and the dependent infant at the other. We don't expect babies to show any signs of responsibility, but as infants grow into childhood we offer them more independence and responsibility. In this way they move away from dependence to embrace more opportunities to become responsible. We may ask them to put away their toys or allow them to choose what they wear. Many children are called on to do household chores, thereby contributing to the well-being of the family.

As children approach preschool and kindergarten, they are given more responsibility. They learn how to be on time for school and may have homework they need to keep track of. Some children are responsible for younger brothers and sisters. As parents and teachers, we celebrate their growth in responsibility.

During the teen years, more independence—and concomitant responsibility—is offered; sometimes this is taken and sometimes not. Teenagers may behave responsibly to maintain a position on a sports team while they ignore the responsibility of completing class projects. They may be quick to take responsibility for their own transportation—whether it is having a bus pass, walking to a friend's house, getting a ride from a classmate, or possibly caring for their own car. At the same time they forget to let their parents know where they are, stay out after curfew, and sneak into R-rated movies. Teenagers may abuse the responsibility they are offered in an effort to test boundaries, wondering what will happen if they don't behave responsibly. The teen years are often a chaotic mix of responsible and irresponsible behavior.

The teen years are often a chaotic mix of responsible and irresponsible behavior.

As young adults, we take on more responsibility by finding work, marrying, and renting or buying our own homes. At some point we become responsible for our own lives as well as becoming responsible for the lives of others. Along with the possibility of raising children, we may gain added responsibility in relation to caring for aging parents, a sibling, or another relative in need. It seems that adding more responsibility to our lives never ends.

Moving from one end of the continuum toward the other is not a solitary journey or a one-way street. It is done in the context of families, schools, work, and communities. Along the way there are bumps and setbacks, obstacles and disappointments, bad choices, and lost dreams. I like to imagine that parents, teachers, coaches, and employers are at the responsible end of the continuum, urging young people toward greater independence, encouraging and rewarding them as they take on more and more responsibility.

However, there is a problem with this picture, for if everyone in the system ends up at one end of the continuum it will go out of balance. To achieve and maintain balance, all participants in the family, classroom, or organization need to be willing to move. If teachers or the ones in charge of the learning group or organization stay firmly rooted to the responsible position, holding tightly to what they perceive is their

> Even when all choices are taken from us, we still have the choice of how to be.

responsibility for the teaching-learning process, students will stop moving. They are waiting for those in charge to make room for them. If teachers are willing to let go of being solely responsible, the students can continue to move forward until teachers and students meet in the middle, the place of balance, interdependence, and shared responsibility. This movement toward the center is what Steve means by the gradual release of responsibility.

The challenge of sharing responsibility in the teaching-learning process in classrooms, workplaces, or with individuals is that parents, teachers, and supervisors must be willing to change their behavior. We cannot share responsibility with our students without letting go of some of our own.

LETTING GO BY OFFERING CHOICES

Middle school teacher Greg Simmons got tired of hearing his students denying their personal responsibility when they said things like "He made me do it," "It's not my fault," "I did what I was told," or "I had no choice." Greg agrees with Viktor Frankl, the father of existential psychology, who taught in *Man's Search for Meaning* that we always have a choice. Even when all choices are taken from us, we still have the choice of how to be.[2]

To teach his students this somewhat abstract concept, Greg invented a role-playing activity to help them see they had options in any given situation. "I would begin by presenting them with a fairly simple and common occurrence, such as noticing that a fellow student was looking at and copying their answers during a test," he told me. "Then the class was challenged to come up with as many responses as possible." Some of the ideas he elicited were "Tell the teacher," "Cover my paper," "Confront the cheater," "Make my answers wrong," "Cooperate," and "Do nothing."

As students continued to present new possibilities, their ideas were not evaluated. Greg simply wrote them all down. The object was to get many choices before them. Later the class would discuss and analyze possible consequences of the different suggested responses. It was hard for the students not to search for the "right" answer and to stay with the process of looking at the many choices they had.

Sometimes the class would puzzle over how a particular behavior might be influenced by the situation, such as the cheater being a best friend, or a bully, or if they had cheated off the friend's paper earlier. They also realized that any choice would lead to further choices. If they were to confront the cheater, would they whisper softly during the test, decide to talk about it later, or maybe even shout out something like this: "Stop looking at my paper, you lousy cheater."

Greg would involve the class in this role-playing activity almost every week. He presented more challenging situations as the months went by. He noticed how the students became more skilled at thinking of options and more thoughtful as they analyzed consequences. He encouraged the students to look at the choices they faced every day in other realms of life, reminding them that no matter how powerless they might feel, they always had some choice.

Greg had two favorite stories that showed how these role-playing activities were brought into the students' everyday lives. One time, after an angry confrontation with a student, the teenager shouted at him, "I didn't choose to be in this class." To which Greg responded just as loudly, "And I didn't choose you as a student, either." They glared at each other and then Greg broke the silence by saying, "We're stuck with each other. Now what choices do we have?" Another time after something had happened in a different classroom, Greg heard one student mutter to her friend, "There were other ways to respond to that teacher, and you sure as hell didn't think of any of them!"

There is always the possibility that too many choices can paralyze students or learners. It is wise to begin with either/or choices, such as, "Do you want to read or play tether ball during recess?" "Do you want to work with this group or work alone?" As students become more comfortable with either/or options, we might then offer them more options, but still impose some limits. "For your final project you can write a research paper or a short story, prepare a video, or come up with another idea that will let me know what you have learned this semester." If we offer wide-open choices, such as "What do you want to do today?" I believe we are no longer sharing responsibility; we are abdicating responsibility.

Limiting choices is also wise in a variety of situations. When my younger stepson Paul was a senior in high school and was faced with choosing where to apply to college, he was overwhelmed by the possibilities. Although he definitely wanted to go to the West Coast and attend a college that was at least as big and diverse as his inner city high school, he seemed unable to think beyond that.

His father and I decided to narrow his options by listing all the colleges within those parameters that we thought he could get into and that we would feel good about his attending. Jim made appointments to visit the campuses that fit the criteria and off they went, starting in southern California and moving north.

Paul is a very sensate and intuitive learner, and we trusted that as he visited these colleges he would know which place was right for him. After four different college tours, all of which were of no interest to him, he arrived at a campus and wasn't there very long before he said, "This is it." He was so sure, they canceled the rest of the visits and flew home. Was it the right choice? Always hard to tell, but it was a good choice, and it was his.

When we offer choices to our children, students, or employees, we need to be sure we are willing to let them live with their choices. Offering options, and then not allowing them to carry out the choice, undermines their trust in us and in themselves. When we know what we want them to do, it is better to tell them that clearly. They still have a choice about how they will respond to our demands.

> By giving children the opportunity to make choices in various areas of their lives, from seemingly small things to the larger ones with more consequences, we are empowering them…. We are leading them from powerlessness to self-determination.

By giving children the opportunity to make choices in various areas of their lives, from seemingly small things to the larger ones with more consequences, we are empowering them. We are not giving up our authority, but rather inviting students into the process of claiming their own authority. We are leading them from powerlessness to self-determination. As we guide our students in this process, it is wise for us to remember the choices we have as teachers. We may not like the subject we have been assigned to teach, we might be unhappy with the size of our classes, or we might prefer to have a different colleague next door. These difficulties can make us feel powerless. Although we may not be offered many choices due to the school leadership, the population we serve, or budget constraints, we can decide for ourselves how we will respond to our disappointments. We have more power over our own lives than we sometimes think.

REIMAGINING POWER

Earlier in this chapter I envisioned power as being hierarchical, with those in power at the top, and those without power at the bottom. In that model, power is experienced as finite, a certain fixed amount of power that cannot be expanded. Imagine for a moment that power resides in separate pieces and that in any situation—a school, a classroom, an organization, a family—there are just one hundred pieces of power to go around. Whoever has the most pieces is in control. If I am that person, I want to hang onto the power I have. I get nervous if I only have fifty-one pieces, so I do everything I can to protect what I have and watch for any opportunity to take power pieces away from others.

One thing I could do is make sure that the other people who have a small number of pieces do not join together to combine their limited power. If they were to do this, my power would be threatened. Therefore, I would separate and isolate people to prevent this from happening. Another tactic would be to take pieces of power from some of the weaker members of the group, diminishing their power and enhancing my own. As I gather more pieces of power, I want to guard that power zealously. I might do that by making myself unavailable, avoiding individual communication, and withholding important information.

But what if power were infinite, rather than finite? What if power were like love and the more you gave away the more you received? In this model, power would no longer reside in the pieces, but in the connections and relationships of the people in the organization who all have at their core their own personal power. Power would no longer be consolidated at the top, but be in constant movement, flowing to and from and through everyone who is connected in a giant web. There would no longer be any need to steal power from others or protect what power we have, for there is more than enough to go around.

Kevin Jackson was blessed to teach in a community college that exemplified this model of infinite power. In his orientation the first week he was at work, the head of the college defined her role as facilitating relationships of support among the faculty. She saw herself as a resource to be called upon as questions arose regarding curriculum, methodologies, and evaluation procedures.

As Kevin got to know the other faculty members in his department, he was amazed at the collaboration and creativity that was generated by working together. He was invited into his colleagues' classrooms to observe and learn, and the other teachers asked him to share his ideas. The head of the college was on the campus much of the time, stopping by department meetings and classrooms, not to evaluate, but to offer guidance and encouragement.

When she called a large faculty meeting, it was not to disseminate information, which she saw as a waste of time, for that could be done electronically. She expected the faculty to be diligent in keeping up with the announcements she sent and she also expected the teachers to keep her informed about what was going on in their classrooms and departments. Communication flowed in both directions. When she did gather the teachers together, it was for the purpose of sharing visions and goals, what was going well, and problem areas that the community might address. The principal's philosophy was that the purpose of meetings was to exchange exciting new ideas, to engage in problem solving, and to connect to others in the wider community.

Kevin said that this sharing of power and his own sense of empowerment flowed into the classroom. Because of how he was being treated, he was able to relate to his students with the same amount of respect he was receiving. The creative energy of the campus environment was experienced by everyone.

Fast-forward a few years, when the head of the campus left for another position and a new chief administrator arrived. Within a few months the environment began to change. The new administrator spent most of her time in her office, guarded by a secretary and a closed door. She informed teachers that department meetings would be suspended in favor of regular full faculty meetings where information flowed only in one direction—from the top down. She encouraged teachers to compete with each other for special recognition.

Kevin said it was as if a balloon had popped and all the good energy that was keeping it aloft dissipated. The collegiality between faculty members vanished. The trust and respect that had previously been present were no longer there. As teacher morale suffered, classrooms were not as lively and creative as they had been. "Everything fell flat," Kevin reported. "It was no longer much fun to go to work."

Most issues of power in classrooms, schools, and other institutions are not as clear-cut as Kevin's story suggests. He experienced how the community college went from a philosophy of infinite power to one where power was limited. But he could not tell us how the original head of the campus created such an environment because it was in place when he arrived.

I imagine it took a long time, a lot of misunderstandings and confusion, and much dialogue to convince the teachers that she meant what she said. Most likely, many of them had never before experienced an environment built around the understanding that power is truly infinite.

If the person in charge wants to teach and lead from the assumption that power lies in relationship, rather than in discrete pieces of power, she finds it difficult if others do not share her view. Students or employees who are used to operating within a hierarchical model may see her as a weak leader, and think she is abdicating her responsibilities. She may be forced back into the hierarchical model if the power she offers is not accepted or is collected rather than passed on. Although she may experience the power that can grow through relationship, those she is leading and teaching are still thinking that power is in the pieces. If they grab what is offered, hoard it, and then build coalitions to increase their collective power, she could be rendered powerless.

Creating a classroom, school, place of business, or family unit based on the belief that power is infinite needs to be done slowly, with careful attention to everyone's readiness to accept this approach. Gradual releasing of responsibility is one practical way this happens. Steve may never have thought about power being infinite, but the way he slowly and carefully shared responsibility with his students indicates that he was operating under that principle. By giving power to his students, his authority and his power to influence grew.

FINDING YOUR OWN WAY TO BE IN CHARGE

Just as we all find our own ways to express kindness and respect to our students, we can find our own style of classroom management. You need not try to become Steve in his fourth-grade classroom or model yourself after any of the other teachers you have been meeting in this book. True authority does not come from copying the way others influence their students or from reading what the experts say about classroom management. These examples and other techniques and guidelines can be helpful as we find our own way, but ultimately our authority comes from within and is expressed through our own unique personality. In addition, without losing our authenticity, we need to find a way to monitor our behavior in response to the particular students we are teaching that year. We all know that what was effective one year or in one class may not work in a different situation.

High school English teacher Peter Baer told me that his voice of authority had to change, not only in relation to his students but also in relation to the ethos of the particular school in which he was teaching. In one school he was supposed to give his students only very limited choices, while in another sharing responsibility through wide-open choices was encouraged. He had to forge his own way in the midst of often conflicting ideas and needs.

"What I have discovered is that the only way to maintain my own authority is to keep alert for what is needed in a particular situation and learn from the times I get it wrong," he told me. He went on to describe a terribly difficult day when he felt his students were taking advantage of him and the open way he was running the class. As their irresponsible behavior increased, he became more and more frustrated. "I lost it," he confessed. "I shouted at them and told them how awful they were. I went on and on about how their actions would lead them to failure. I even told them I was ready to give up on them. At which point I left the classroom and slammed the door."

Peter stayed in the hallway outside the classroom trying to pull himself together. He realized that the students had been shocked into silence by his outburst. At the same time he knew that yelling and blaming were not how he wanted to relate to his students in his attempt to maintain order. He saw that beneath his anger was a deep disappointment that his students were not willing to share responsibility for their own learning.

> "That day was a turning point in understanding how my inner life affects my presence in the classroom."

Maybe he needed to let go of that precious belief and find another way to empower his students. So, taking a deep breath, he opened the door and reentered the classroom. He apologized for his behavior and told the class that the teacher they had just witnessed was not the man he wanted to be and that he would try not to let it happen again.

"I don't think it is a bad thing for teenagers to see their teacher as a real human being who gets frustrated and explodes in anger," he said. "I also believe that expressing my anger without hurting anyone, and apologizing afterward, modeled ways they could manage their own anger. In many ways it was a horrible day, but we all recovered. I wonder if the students remember it as vividly as I do. That day was a turning point in understanding how my inner life affects my presence in the classroom."

Looking Inward, Going Deeper

1. What has been your experience of shared responsibility in the classroom or with individual students? How has it worked for you? Where have problems arisen?

2. As you think of the two models of power we have explored, allow images to emerge from your mind and heart for each of the models, and draw them. What do

you learn from this visual aid? How might it guide you in claiming your own authority?

3. Describe how you claim authority in the classroom, in your place of business, on the sports field, or any other place you hold the designated or informal position of teacher. How has your approach to claiming authority evolved over your years of teaching?

CHAPTER SIX

ATTENDING TO OUR INNER LANDSCAPE

SEEING, EMBRACING, AND TRANSFORMING OUR SHADOWS

*When I looked at what I had drawn in meditation,
I realized I was turning my life over to the
expectations of others.*

Elizabeth Jones

T he spiritual leadership workshop that middle school teacher Elizabeth Jones attended was designed to help participants explore their inner landscapes as a way to uncover the hidden parts of themselves that might keep them from being the authentic teachers they hoped to be. The eighteen who gathered formed a supportive community in which to engage in meditation, guided imagery, journaling, and deep listening, as well as music, movement, and art. Although we often believe that exploring our inner lives is a solitary activity, the participants soon realized how valuable trusted companions could be in this journey.

In this particular exercise, the leader invited each of the participants to find a comfortable place in the room with their drawing materials nearby. They were then asked to close their eyes and pay attention to their breathing. After a few moments they were instructed to pay attention to their bodies, notice what was present, and accept whatever they experienced as part of this moment. After another pause they were to pay attention to their feelings and their thoughts in the same pattern of noticing and accepting.

"Now allow the physical, emotional, and mental experiences to slide to the periphery of your mind and heart," the leader said. "And in the inner space that appears, imagine yourself in your leadership position. Notice if you are in a particular building or room, maybe outdoors, or even on the move. When you are ready, begin to surround that picture of yourself with the expectations of others. These expectations may come in images, words, or just as a felt sense. Pay attention to how you feel as you recognize the many expectations that are present in your leadership arena. In your mind's eye, allow an image to emerge of you trying to meet all those demands."

The leader told them to take all the time they needed to explore this new image. When they were ready, they were to bring their attention back to the room and pick up their crayons to sketch an image of themselves in that particular situation. The room was filled with silent creative energy as crayons were put to paper. As they drew, the participants created images that might offer a new awareness of ways their inner lives could be affecting their leading and teaching.

The image Elizabeth drew was a female figure with a blank, emotionless face and eight elongated arms, stretched out in all directions. Her hands were open, and she seemed to be floating in space. She saw how ungrounded she was and how her face indicated an absence of excitement and purpose. She interpreted the many arms and open hands as the way she was always looking outside herself, grasping for guidance and approval. When she shared her drawing with a partner, he asked her if she thought maybe the open hands also signified how she was giving herself away to all the expectations others had of her.

Elizabeth's initial response to the image and her partner's insight was sadness. That feeling is not uncommon as we turn our gaze inward, for often what we discover undermines our understanding of the person we believe ourselves to be. Elizabeth thought of herself as a well-grounded woman, making decisions and taking action congruent with her inner guidance. This new image told her that that might not always be the case. She wondered which image was true.

EMBRACING OUR SHADOWS

When we discover something in our own being that is counter to who we think we are, we often move quickly from sadness to judgment. Elizabeth didn't like what she saw in her drawing, although she recognized that it represented a part of who she was. When she shared her feelings with the whole group, she wondered what she could do to get rid of her tendency to turn her life over to others' expectations. The leader's response was startling: "You must embrace the image and treat it with kindness and respect."

> We cannot change anything we do not first accept.

There is a well-known saying in psychospiritual work that we cannot change anything we do not first accept. As counterintuitive as that may seem, I know it is true. In Elizabeth's case, she needed to welcome the stranger represented by her drawing and see what wisdom it had to offer. This wasn't easy, for she didn't like the blank face and the many arms and open hands. The image made her feel uncomfortable and ashamed of herself.

However, when she stayed with her inner work, noticing her feelings and thoughts, she realized that both images of herself were true. She is the well-grounded woman living from her own inner truths *and* she is the woman who gets caught up in trying to meet other people's needs. When she stepped back for a wider view, she saw that,

> Embracing the shadow side of ourselves leads to transformation by breaking open our previous self-image.

although she is grounded and clear about her values, becoming aware of other people's expectations is important in her role as a teacher. These expectations, if they do not capture her, give her a context for the teaching-learning process. By listening to the ideas of others and sorting through which expectations might be helpful, she could choose those she wanted to incorporate into her teaching. If she hung on too tightly to her strong self-image, ignoring the expectations around her, she might block the growth that comes with new ideas.

All of us are surrounded by the expectations of others, no matter what our position. In elementary school the students may expect us to make all of learning fun, while many parents want us to get their children up to grade level in every subject. In secondary school there is the pressure to raise the graduation numbers, and in graduate school we are expected to be scholars and writers as well as capable teachers. Sometimes when we mentor or do consulting, we are expected to work miracles. And in all situations the surrounding communities are filled with conflicting expectations!

I imagine we all feel a little like Elizabeth, pulled off our center when we try to meet everyone's needs. If we recognize this tendency in ourselves and embrace it as an integral part of who we are, we will be free to choose which expectations to honor and which to let slide. We cannot experience this freedom without first seeing what is going on within and accepting it respectfully as part of who we are. Embracing the shadow side of ourselves leads to transformation by breaking open our previous self-image and allowing us to become more authentic than we were before.

PAYING ATTENTION TO OUR INNER LANDSCAPE LEADS TO AUTHENTICITY

Elizabeth's inner work was stimulated by a guided meditation in a workshop, but that is not the only way to tap into our inner lives. If we are mindful and willing to look, we are given clues all the time about what is going on within. If we recognize and honor our feelings, we may discover some hidden and valuable information.

Sam Martinez, an experienced fifth-grade teacher, was growing anxious as the new school year approached. This was not like him, for in the past he had awaited a new group of students with eager anticipation and excitement. He wondered what was prompting this unfamiliar anxiety. On his early morning walk a few weeks before school started, the name and face of a recently retired colleague suddenly came to mind. He thought about what a fine teacher she was, and how parents and students alike adored her. Then it dawned on him. He was comparing himself to her and beginning to compete with her. She had taught the students he was to teach this year, and he was feeling that he would be a great disappointment to them.

When he recognized the source of his anxiety, he was able to work with his discovery. "I don't usually think of myself as a competitive person," he told me, "but I had to accept that comparing and competing were the basis of my anxiety." When he identified and accepted this pattern, he saw his own strengths and competencies apart from his colleague's. He was sure his students would miss her, but he knew that he had his own unique gifts to offer them. He acknowledged that competition was part of his nature and could be a gift, for in the past it had led him to work toward becoming a better teacher. But in this situation his competitive side had grown so strong it was making him anxious. By paying attention to his anxiety and uncovering its source, he was able to free himself to be the very best teacher he could be. "If I hadn't seen what was going on," he told me, "I could have wasted a lot of energy trying to be better than her, rather than being myself."

When we have the courage to look at ourselves in our complexity, we are doing what British biologist Thomas Huxley advised: "Sit down before fact as a little child, be prepared to give up every preconceived notion, follow humbly wherever and to whatever abyss nature leads, or you shall learn nothing."[1] When Elizabeth and Sam followed this guidance, they learned more about who they were. At first they resisted what they saw and were hesitant to embrace their shadows. Soon, however, they realized that, by trying to rid themselves of behaviors and attitudes they didn't initially like, they would be diminishing themselves, instead of growing into who they were called to be.

COMMON SHADOWS IN TEACHERS' LIVES

As teachers, I believe we are called to regularly engage our inner lives, to recognize our shadows and do the brave work of embracing them. We can then be open to their gifts and welcome the possibility of transformation. We all have our own stories and their accompanying shadows, based on our family and culture of origin, early experiences, age, geographical location, and myriad other factors. In addition to what we discover through our individual work, I have noticed a few common shadows that many teachers share;

these get in the way of engaging fully in the sacred art of teaching. The ones we will explore are striving for perfection, fearing interruptions and surprise, and believing our own and other's projections.

STRIVING FOR PERFECTION

"Flawless" is what we usually mean when we use the word *perfect*. As impossible as that is in most areas of life, the desire for perfection seduces everyone at some time or another. As teachers, the attempt to be perfect robs us of our willingness to make mistakes, which in turn keeps us from trying new ways of teaching, meeting student needs in creative ways, or being spontaneous in the middle of a carefully structured lesson. We attempt to handle everything with no errors in our speech or behavior. This longing for perfection is one of the shadows that can undermine our authenticity.

The desire for perfection seduces everyone at some time or another.

However, if we understand *perfection* to mean "excellence," this striving can encourage us to do our best, watch for ways to improve our lessons and our relationship to students, and be gentle with ourselves when we make mistakes. I find it easy to slide from the energizing search for excellence to the futile experience of longing for flawlessness. Attention to the inner life helps us notice when this begins to happen.

Our confusion about perfection may stem from a common source that lies within the Christian Scriptures. This writing seems to influence our thinking and behavior no matter what our faith or lack of faith. In the Gospel of Matthew it is written, "Be perfect, therefore, as your heavenly Father is perfect" (5:48). In other words, be without defect or blemish. What a tall order!

Kathleen Norris, a theologian and poet, writes about how this verse has permeated our culture. "Perfectionism has become a marked characteristic of contemporary American culture and is one of the scariest words I know."[2] When we strive for perfection, we are constantly trying to reach some imaginary and unattainable standard. Finding ourselves always failing to measure up, we are constantly concerned with our self-image, a preoccupation that can stunt emotional and spiritual growth.[3]

She goes on to say, "The good news about the word 'perfect' as used in the Christian Scriptures is that it is not a scary word, so much as a scary translation."[4] By this she means that a more accurate translation would call us not to be perfect, but to be complete, whole, fully grown, or mature. In other words, to become who we are meant to be.

To let go of our striving for flawlessness, we must first acknowledge that it is part of our makeup, although we would prefer not to admit it. We might often say scornfully of another, "She is such a perfectionist." But if we are able to move our gaze from the other to our own inner landscape, we will

> "The good news about the word 'perfect' as used in the Christian Scriptures is that it is not a scary word, so much as a scary translation."

probably find lurking in the shadows our own desire to be perfect. Our task is to recognize and embrace this longing so that we can strive instead to do well, become competent, and keep learning. Teaching from that place is a totally different experience than trying to teach perfectly.

Not only is striving for flawless perfection a danger to our own souls, but also demanding perfection from our students can paralyze them. There are some instances when students must be judged on how close they have come to perfection, as in medicine, chemical equations, or building plans. But much of learning calls our students to engagement, rather than perfection.

Jennifer Friedman, a student in my seminary class on spiritual practices, was a teacher of Dances of Universal Peace. She volunteered to guide the class in an experience of this embodied form of prayer. Many of the students were hesitant, feeling awkward in

> Much of learning calls our students to engagement, rather than perfection.

their bodies and remembering embarrassing times in their past when they were expected to dance. But they all agreed to participate, and the next half hour was an experience of masterful teaching.

Jennifer acknowledged their hesitancy, showed us a few simple steps, and reassured us that getting the dance right was not the point. What was important was our attitude of exploration and the desire to dance for peace. What fun we had! We stumbled and laughed. We loosened up and felt joy in our bodies. She added song and a few sang and danced at the same time.

In the discussion afterward, I asked the students what allowed them to learn so quickly. They responded, "She was so relaxed," "It was clear she knew what she was doing," "She never pointed out mistakes," "She was having fun," and "She didn't care if we did it perfectly." I intervened at this point and said, "Imagine what this last half hour would have been like if Jennifer had tried to get us to do the steps right, if the goal had been to dance perfectly." I watched as their bodies stiffened and the excitement drained from their faces. They experienced how harsh it feels when teachers demand unnecessary perfection.

In learning to become a yoga teacher, Mark, whom we met in Chapter 1, noticed that the emphasis was always on attempting to perfect the various poses, as though that would somehow bring on enlightenment. He realized that demanding perfect form distracted his students from focusing on the present moment because they believed that perfection would occur at some unspecified point in the future. Pushing students toward a level of practice that was unattainable caused them to be displeased with who they were and what they could do in the moment. "I want people to love themselves just as they are, and if they want to go further in a pose, they can do so with relaxation, breathing, meditation, and love," he said. "Life is too short to focus our study and our practice on perfection."

Closely akin to striving for perfection is the compulsion to become an expert in one's field. Being an expert is not in itself a problem. Remember Peter Schneider's paradoxical words at the beginning of Chapter 3: "Because I am an expert in my field, I can afford to let go and approach my subject with all the passion of a beginner." Peter embodies the wisdom of Shunryu Suzuki, a Soto Zen monk and teacher, who wrote, "In the beginner's mind there are many possibilities. In the expert's mind there are few."[5] Peter is the expert who has mastered his field of study; at the same time he possesses a beginner's mind that allows him great freedom to explore all options and possibilities within his area of expertise. The problem comes when we live out only half of that paradox. By concentrating on becoming an expert, we may begin to identify with the depth and breadth of our knowledge, rather than attending to our connection with the wonder of the content we are teaching and the importance of the relationship we have with our students.

When we put all our energy into the opposite side of the paradox, teaching only from the beginner's mind, we may discount and withhold what we know. My friend Susan told me how amazed she was that people kept hiring her as a consultant. When she asked someone why he wanted her to work with him, he replied that it was because of her expertise and her teaching skills. "I've never thought of myself as an expert," she told me. "Maybe it is time to recognize my accomplishments." Susan tried out that self-affirmation. "I am an expert!" she said. And then she smiled. "I am also twelve years old." Through her examination of her inner landscape, Susan had arrived, like Peter, at the place of both/and rather than either/or—she celebrates her beginner's mind while also sharing her gifts and talents.

FEARING INTERRUPTIONS AND SURPRISE

Do you like surprises? Do you resist them or welcome them? I was given a surprise party on my eighteenth birthday and I hated it. I had been invited on a fancy date by a boy I really liked, and I was so excited to spend my special day with him. After he picked me up, we stopped by another friend's house for him to drop something off. He told me it might take a few minutes, so he asked me to go in with him. As I walked in the door, twenty people jumped out from hiding places screaming, "Surprise!"

The whole evening was a blur. I couldn't orient myself to what was happening. Why wasn't I on my highly anticipated date? Why was everyone so excited? How was I supposed to act? What I really wanted to do was go in a room, close the door, and cry. My birthday had not turned out as well as my friends had hoped. For me it was a disaster.

By being surprised, I had missed the pleasure of the planning and anticipation of the celebration. Whether it is a dinner party, a trip, or the first day of school, I love the time of preparation. I focus on practical plans and details, as well as picturing in my mind and heart the living out of what I have planned. I also know that when I am confronted with the unexpected, as I was at eighteen, I am no longer in control. I am confused and don't know what to do; I feel as if I have no choice and that some outside force has thrown me off balance. When I spoke to my spiritual director about my fear of surprise and how I try to protect myself, he suggested that in doing so I was defending myself from being vulnerable and open to the spirit.

Writer, speaker, and activist Parker J. Palmer uses different words to express the same idea. He believes that when we lose our capacity for surprise we diminish our ability to know, teach, and learn.[6] Our task as teachers is to honor the fear we have of the unexpected as an integral part of our humanness. When we embrace that fear, we can listen to it as a way to protect ourselves from real danger, at the same time becoming open to the possibility of welcoming surprises that may guide us into new insights, experiences, and possibilities. "Life catches us by surprise. Frees us by surprise," declares Trappist monk Brother David Steindl-Rast.[7]

To welcome the unexpected is not the same as living and teaching in an unsettled environment. When everything around us is chaotic, we experience disorder and confusion. Nothing is certain; there is only surprise. Without guidelines, boundaries, and order, we are so focused on trying to find our way and stay upright that we have no desire for more surprise. Many of our students live in such an environment and I believe they long for some structure, a place where they feel safe. As teachers, it is our responsibility to create that space for them and for us. Then the surprises that do break in can be welcomed and explored.

When the environment is stable and we have honored our fear, we can support our students when they are surprised and knocked off balance and also handle the students surprising us with their behavior or their ideas. As teachers, we can also be alert to times when we surprise ourselves by saying something we had never thought of before or being stumped by a student's original and evocative question. Surprising our students by breaking patterns or acting in new ways can be great fun. My fifth-grade teacher, Mrs. Rust, would sometimes stop us in the middle of a difficult lesson, saying, "Put away your books and let's sing." She would sit down at the old upright piano in the classroom and vigorously pound out popular songs that we all knew.

We can be afraid and welcoming, defensive and open, and when we realize this we can be more spontaneous in the teaching-learning process. Annabel Hue, a third-grade teacher in California, spoke of the time that a freak dust storm moved through the playground of the school. The students rushed to the window to watch this astonishing occurrence. "It was wonderful," she said. "It raised all sorts of questions about wind and weather that we could explore together as a class." She learned later that the teacher next door told the students to stay in their seats as she pulled the drapes shut and continued with her planned lesson.

Wonder is the by-product of welcoming surprise for both the teacher and the learner, and it is what makes teaching a sacred art. With Annabel's response to the dust storm, she was teaching more than the origins and behavior of wind. She was teaching her students about greeting the world with wonder. Annabel was letting them see that wonder could be a response to everything in their lives. She was offering them the experience of what Jewish scholar and twentieth-century theologian Abraham Joshua Heschel called "radical amazement."[8]

BELIEVING OUR OWN AND OTHERS' PROJECTIONS

Projections occur when your inner life—past experiences, present feelings, or hopes for the future—influences your perception of this moment's reality. Maybe you had a bossy older brother whose treatment of you was disturbing and you never dealt with your feelings. In your adult life, bossy boys and men give rise to resentment—not just because they are actually overbearing but also because they remind you of your brother and the pain of growing up. You may project your unacknowledged resentment onto these males and respond to their behavior from the place of the young child. When this happens you are not seeing these people—students, colleagues, or students' parents—for who they truly are. Your perception of them is colored by your feelings and past experiences of your overbearing sibling.

Projection work brings to awareness feelings and parts of ourselves that we have rejected and sent into the shadows. When we do this work successfully, we are able to engage in honest communication and dialogue with students, colleagues, and parents. When conferring with the mother of one of my students, I realized that I was angry with her, felt no compassion toward her, and became very judgmental of her. I dreaded our meetings and frequently anticipated the negative energy I knew I would experience when we were together. When I told a friend, who was also a therapist, the trouble I was having with her, he asked me if she reminded me of myself. "Absolutely not," I cried defensively. "She is dependent and always looking for someone either to blame for her troubles or to rescue her."

Wonder is the by-product of welcoming surprise for both the teacher and the learner.

The energy of my response indicated that my wise friend might have touched on a hidden truth. In reflection I had to recognize the dependent part of myself that I had been ignoring and judging as I was growing in my strength and independence. In truth, there was still a dependent woman inside me who was longing to be taken care of. As I embraced this inner need, I was able to realize that in my wholeness there was room for both parts of myself. I was dependent as well as strong and independent. I didn't need to give up one to become the other. I could celebrate that I embodied both. This inner work freed me to relate to this student's mother with compassion. It changed the whole relationship.

Parker J. Palmer writes of his own work with projection. "As I teach, I project the condition of my soul onto my students, their families, and on our way of being together. The entanglements in the classroom are often no more or less than the convolutions of my inner life. Viewed from this angle, teaching holds a mirror to my soul."[9] Our task is to look into the mirror to see what is there. Peter Baer looked into that

> Projection work brings to awareness feelings and parts of ourselves that we have rejected and sent into the shadows.

mirror as he stood in the hallway after his angry outburst. Elizabeth Jones looked in her mirror as she took her drawing seriously. Sam Martinez looked in his mirror and saw how his unacknowledged competitive streak was making him so anxious about the new school year.

Along with the problematic parts of ourselves, we also can project our hidden gifts onto others. If we find ourselves envious of another's gift, we might look within for that gift in ourselves. I worked with a young priest who noticed how envious he was of his high school students' energy and excitement. "I've lost all that joie de vivre," he said sadly. "I used to have a lot of fun playing at life." It seems that going to seminary and studying for the priesthood turned him into a serious man, focused on his studies and on God. He had left his fun-loving self behind. By looking into the mirror of his soul, he realized that he could forgive himself for abandoning his passion for life and could reclaim the youthful, exuberant teenager within. In doing so, his teaching became livelier and his students began to engage him and the subject with a lightheartedness that had been missing before.

Another way that projections manifest in the teaching-learning process is when students or colleagues ascribe to you their own unrecognized gifts. A staff member at the Iliff School of Theology exclaimed to me years ago, "You are the soul of the seminary!" I am sure she thought she was offering me a compliment, but her statement made me anxious. What if I believed her projection, took on that role, and began acting and teaching from that identity? Acknowledging my fear made me realize the power of projections, not only in an individual life but also in the life of the community.

> Our task is to look into the mirror to see what is there.

A more distressing projection was the unacknowledged anger projected onto Kendra Billings when she was facilitating a small group as part of a weeklong seminar. Suddenly, in what seemed like normal interactions among the participants, a man began criticizing her for her leadership. He was very emotional and was becoming mean. Another member of the group told him that his demeanor and words were inappropriate. At that point he ran from the room.

Kendra was visibly shaken, but managed to continue with the day's agenda. Right before the group was to end, the man came back into the room to apologize. After he left, he had walked around the campus trying to understand what had happened. That angry behavior was not his usual way of responding to others, even in stressful moments. And then it dawned on him! Something Kendra had said reminded him of his ex-wife and their relationship, which was still turbulent and unresolved. All his unexpressed anger spewed forth onto Kendra. He apologized to her and the rest of the group and then broke down in tears. He had the courage to look into his mirror and see himself and Kendra for who they were. He also knew he needed to do some more inner work on the issues raised by his divorce.

Teachers and leaders are lightning rods for other people's projections. As we stand before a classroom or work with learners one-on-one, students are very likely not only seeing us as who we are but also identifying us with other people in their lives—parents, former teachers, movie stars, and characters from novels. Not all these projections have a negative impact, but they do keep teachers and students from forming genuine relationships with one another. There is little we can do to help others recognize the projections they put on us, except to be willing to be as authentic as we can. In this way others are more likely to see us clearly and begin to reclaim the projections they have placed on us.

Closely akin to projecting our inner life onto others is the process of personalizing. When we personalize, we mistakenly believe that everything happening in the outside world is all about us. If your colleague doesn't respond to your email over the weekend, you might think that she is mad at you. You might fret about this for three days, only to discover that her young son had been taken ill on Friday night. Her silence had nothing to do with you.

Poet and teacher Garret Keizer recounts the experience of receiving a poem from a student about how bored she was in his English class. "Are my feelings hurt?" he writes. "A little I suppose. But I've taught long enough to know that these affronts are almost never personal in the strictest sense. They have to do with the needs and grievances way beyond any teacher's powers of interpretation."[10]

Being Realistic

You will never completely stop personalizing the outside world, reclaim your projections, confront all your shadows, or clear out all the cobwebs lingering in the corners of your inner landscape. However, self-exploration will help you recognize disappointments, unrealistic expectations, hidden prejudices, and insecurities that keep you from bringing your authentic self into the teacher-learner relationship. As you explore these traps or detours, remember that they are a natural part of the process of discovering who you are. As you meet them, experience them, and feel them, you may learn more about your vulnerabilities and strengths that can lead you more deeply into your own self-knowledge. "Good teaching," declares Parker J. Palmer, "requires self-knowledge: It is a secret hidden in plain sight."[11]

Looking Inward, Going Deeper

1. Using the guidelines on pages 91–92, envision a part of yourself that is often controlled by others' expectations. Draw the image and see how it may block your authenticity. Also take note of what gifts it may bring.

2. Where in your life are you seduced by the idea of becoming flawless and perfect? How does that longing get in the way of your teaching authentically? What might happen if excellence, rather than perfection, were guiding you? Might you then relax and recognize the strength and competence that you already possess?

3. As a way to explore how you might guard against surprise, stand with your feet slightly apart and your knees unlocked. Using your arms and upper body, move yourself into a defensive position. This might be

by crossing your arms tightly across your chest or your belly. From this pose, say to yourself, "I will not be surprised, I will not be surprised, I will not be surprised." Then take a deep breath, feel your feet on the floor giving you steady support, stand up straight, opening your eyes and arms, and say to yourself a number of times, "I welcome the surprises life brings." Describe the physical and corresponding emotional difference in the two positions. How might this be useful in your teaching life?

4. When have you experienced teaching as holding a mirror to your soul? Describe the situation in detail. What feelings arise? What did you learn?

CHAPTER SEVEN

TEACHING
WHO WE ARE
HONORING OUR UNIQUE GIFTS

Rosemarie helped me to discover my deepest calling.
Dr. Vincent Harding

African-American historian and scholar Vincent Harding always began his classes and lectures with this question: "Who was your mama's mama, and where did she come from?" If the group was small enough, we all went around the circle to share our mother's mother's name and where she was born. In a larger lecture or presentation, he would invite six or seven people to come forward and share. For people who did not know Vincent, this seemed like a strange way for a veteran of the civil rights movement, a personal friend of Martin Luther King Jr., and a nationally known community organizer, writer, and teacher to begin any class. But that question to his students and audiences was the essence of who he was.

Vincent grew up an only child of a single mother, and he recognized and honored the power of the feminine influence in his life and in all our lives. His opening question helped us connect to our maternal lineage and guide us to an understanding that who we are today has a lot to do with where we came from. This, in turn, helps us know where we are going.

"Uncle Vincent," as young people called him, was a master teacher of people of all ages. He would get down on the floor with young children and ask them questions about their lives. He listened closely to their stories and asked questions that would deepen the telling. He did this with adults as well.

During the question-and-answer period held after my presentation on spiritual practices at a large American Baptist church, many questions were asked of me that I was quick to answer. Toward the end of the period of dialogue, Vincent, who was sitting off to the side of the sanctuary, stood up slowly. In his large yet soft voice, he greeted me, saying, "Sister Jane. I have learned much about you this evening that I didn't know, but there is one thing I am curious about." He paused. "Could you tell me how you have come to hold such an inclusive Christian belief?"

His was such a soulful question that I responded, "I can, Vincent, but it will take me a minute." He stood, waiting patiently, until I found the words to respond, and he remained standing as I spoke from my heart, realizing I was saying something to that crowd of people I had never said before. Through questions like this one, Vincent brought forth the depth and possibility he recognized in everyone. His carefully crafted questions came from his deep listening and his loving heart. Vincent, the perennial learner, was teaching who he was, thus becoming an agent of change in many lives.

This gentle questioning was not always Vincent's teaching style. As a young social activist, he proclaimed many ideas and strategies for nonviolent resistance. He was skilled at analyzing situations, telling people what more they needed to do beyond what they were doing, and what they weren't doing well. After one such lecture, his wife Rosemarie said, "You are very good at those kinds of things, but I think that what people need more than anything else is encouragement—encouragement to be better than they are. Vincent, I think that you can do a very good job at that."[1] In reflection later in life Vincent said, "In a profound sense, Rosemarie helped me to discover my deepest calling."[2]

THE DEEPEST CALL IS TO BE WHO WE ARE

We started this book exploring the call to teach and the possibility that teaching might become a vocation. Through stories, information, and reflection, we have looked inward, going more deeply into the discovery of who we are not only as teachers but also as women and men for whom teaching is only a part of life. I believe the deepest calling

> I believe the deepest calling ... is the call to be who we truly are.

that Vincent was referring to is the call to be who we truly are. That call is not to leave where we are so we can arrive somewhere else, but rather to look within and surrender to what is already within us, letting go of all that covers up our true self.

This process is not one of struggling and striving to first discover who we are called to be before we bring ourselves to our students. Instead, the many experiences of our vocations can guide us toward a deeper self-understanding. "I have never gone to work in a school with what might be called purity of heart, though much of what I know about purity of heart I learned there," wrote high school English teacher Garret Keizer.[3] I imagine this might be true for all of us, and not just about purity of heart but also about our courage, creativity, vulnerability, and wisdom. I didn't go into teaching knowing who I was. As I look back to those early days, I am aware of how little I knew about myself.

I realize how the years of teaching have provided me with mirrors of self-discovery. I had to pay attention to the lessons that were before me, come out of hiding from behind who I thought I was, and become aware of who I was called to be.

We can see this movement in the lives of the teachers you have met throughout this book. Preaching professor Holly Heuer discovered how the awareness of and her apology for her mistake gave her a new sense of authority. Kristin Waters, a high school principal, realized that, when given the opportunity to work on educational policy and supervision at the district level, her soul was fed by her day-to-day contact with students and teachers. Jessica Yeager learned more about her own love of learning by homeschooling her children.

> The journey to a deepening sense of self is defined by surrender rather than by striving and hard work, even though working with what we discover about ourselves can be difficult.

We live in a culture that encourages us to be ambitious, to struggle to get ahead, and to measure our success against others. But this is not the way of the heart. The journey to a deepening sense of self is defined by surrender, rather than by striving and hard work, even though working with what we discover about ourselves can be difficult, as we witnessed in the stories of the last chapter. Self-knowledge comes slowly, through continually paying attention to our actions, feelings, and thoughts as we go through our days, knowing that every interaction, mistake, success, conflict, and burst of feeling can become our teacher. This awareness of the possibilities of growth and inner knowing that are all around us is what makes teaching a sacred art.

Growing in Integrity and Authenticity

We often think someone either acts with integrity or doesn't; is either authentic or isn't. However, this either/or thinking discounts the process of unfolding, growing, and deepening. Vincent was authentic in his early years of teaching by sharing his passion and urging people to do more for the sake of justice. But over the years and through the perceptive words of a loved one, he realized he was growing into a deeper sense of self. He didn't leave his

> If we are truly ourselves we will be inconsistent, for we are multifaceted and complex human beings.

passion behind. I was witness to his sharp, analytical mind and the forcefulness of what he believed. But as he grew older, he tended more toward gentle questions, simply being with his students and encouraging them not to do what he said but to be true to who they were and to share with the world their unique gifts.

Dana Wilbanks, the professor of religion we met in Chapter 2, started his teaching in exactly the ways he had been taught. By crafting lectures, choosing appropriate reading, and assigning evocative written work, he was being authentic. After realizing that many in the class were not responding the way he had as a student, he sought guidance from colleagues and began to try different teaching methods. Changes in behavior always lead to inner explorations, raising questions like these: "Will I be able to do this?" "What if I fail?" "Who am I becoming if I am no longer who I was?" With the changes in Dana's behavior and by doing the accompanying inner work, he was growing in authenticity.

Being authentic and teaching with integrity do not mean that we finally figure out who we are and then bring ourselves to our teaching with consistent behavior. If we are truly ourselves, we will be inconsistent, for we are multifaceted and complex human beings. Peter Baer acknowledged this when he lost his temper, yelled at his students, and stormed out of the classroom. He knew he was coolheaded in his methods of classroom management, but that day his frustration overwhelmed him. What his students saw was an authentic response to their behavior. Peter brought his whole self into that classroom—frustrations as well as joy. His awareness of what was happening to him and his subsequent conversation modeled for his students the depth of his integrity.

As I look back over my many years of teaching, I can recall how I have brought more of myself to the classroom. Changes in behavior were necessary as I changed from teaching children to teaching adults. My subject matter changed as I moved from leading teacher education classes to teaching courses in prayer and spiritual practice. Each change invited me into new explorations and awareness, leading to greater self-knowledge. I also notice that even without those external changes I learn more about myself and my subject as I engage with different groups of people and have the opportunity to pay attention to my motivations and old habits in a variety of situations. What I see and accept allows me to bring more of myself to the teaching-learning process.

I imagine the same is true for you, whether you are a new teacher or have taught for a long time. Changes in subject matter, grade level, school, district, or other teaching venues bring new opportunities for more self-knowledge. How you taught years ago was probably authentic to who you were and what you knew about yourself at that time. You may look back at some of the ways you behaved in those early situations and wonder, "What was I thinking?" It is wise to be aware of your growth and your authenticity as you teach today, but how you teach now and your deepening self-knowledge do not call you to judge your younger self.

Think back to the teacher in Kristin Waters's high school who resigned, along with many more teachers across the nation, in the fall of the first year of teaching. Those teachers might be harshly judged. People could say they failed because they were unable to complete the job they had been hired to do. But I wonder what the experience taught them about their calling and their identity. It takes a lot of courage to realize you are in the wrong place at the wrong time, and the wisest thing to do is let the commitment go. I believe this reflects deep and true self-knowledge, not failure.

Growing in self-knowledge can be risky and uncomfortable, for you often have to give up who you think you are to become who you truly are. Teachers who leave their positions may need to realize that teaching is not their vocation. This awareness can seem like a dead end, a failed dream, or conjure up feelings of inadequacy, but it may be the beginning of something new and previously unimaginable.

Remember who you were as a teenager, a young adult, or even just five years ago. Are you the same person? Haven't you let go of some behaviors, attitudes, and beliefs, replacing them with new ways of seeing and relating to the world? I imagine that some of your unfolding happened naturally, in response to new responsibilities and roles. Other times your plans may not have materialized and you had to strike out in another direction, not really knowing where you were going. Rather than external events guiding you toward greater self-awareness, you may have gotten in touch with some inner longing that called you to an intentional exploration of your inner landscape. Maybe you began to feel that all was not right in your life, that something was missing, that you could be happier, more competent, or more at peace. I believe these inner promptings come from the depths of who we are—sometimes called our inner wisdom, our soul, or our higher

self—urging us to greater awareness and guiding us to tap
into our unique gifts.

DISCOVERING OUR OWN TREASURES

The ancient Chinese philosopher and poet Lao-Tzu wrote, "I
have just three things to teach: simplicity, patience, compassion. These are your greatest treasures."[4] I believe this ancient
sage is claiming those particular treasures for himself, from his
own experience, and that his call to us is to discover the gifts
inherent in who we are. These treasures will then guide us to
teach who we are no matter what the subject matter or the age
of our students.

The stories of the teachers in the previous chapters reveal
the gifts they possess. In addition to the treasures Lao-Tzu
claims for himself, I see in these teachers the gifts of liberation, love, gratitude, and wisdom, all of which are gifts
of the spirit. As the spirit
moves through our lives,
the gifts flower slowly,
and we often do not recognize how the gifts are
changing us. But if we pay
attention to our motivations, feelings, and behavior, we may see how we have grown.
What used to cause anxiety no longer does so. The people we
formerly judged we now regard with curiosity. We acknowledge mistakes and they do not undermine our sense of competence. Our teaching lives offer us unique opportunities to
accept the mirror that is offered through our daily experiences
of the teaching-learning process. By gazing at and playing in
our inner landscapes, we become clearer about who we are
and what treasures we are bringing into the world. As you
read through the following descriptions of gifts you may be

> By gazing at and playing
> in our inner landscapes, we
> become clearer about who we
> are and what treasures we are
> bringing into the world.

developing—gifts that your students and the world need—notice which ones you identify with and acknowledge that these treasures are yours to share in your own unique way.

Simplicity

We often talk about simplifying our lives, which usually means downsizing and letting go of stuff. This certainly can be important, but in our teaching lives simplicity often has more to do with letting go of plans, expectations, and assumptions. As we do our inner work, we may see where we are holding tight and how that grip is causing us and others to struggle and suffer.

Winston Churchill wrote, "Plans are useless, but planning is invaluable."[5] As teachers, we know how valuable planning is. To go into a classroom, a training session, or a tutorial with no plans is courting disaster. But to hold on to plans that are not working, or plans made without some flexibility, is to miss many a teachable moment. Remember the teacher who drew the drapes when the dust storm swirled by? The interruption may come from a student's evocative and wise question that captures the imagination. It could come from a colleague arriving unexpectedly to show you her new baby. Can we let go of where we thought we were headed and allow the learning to go in a different direction?

Another way to honor simplicity in our teaching is to use fewer words of explanation and to ask more questions.

Another way to honor simplicity in our teaching is to use fewer words of explanation and to ask more questions. In this way we do not go on and on, sharing information that is of no use to the learner and often makes the subject more complex than necessary. I have been brought up short at times when trying to explain a difficult concept in a variety of ways. A student will raise his or her hand and offer a clear, simple, and succinct observation with the words, "Is this what you are trying to say?"

Life, learning, and ideas are complex, and they need to be recognized as such and not discounted. Teaching with simplicity honors the complexity inherent in our subject matter without compounding it. We need to offer explanations as simply as possible, only adding more words as questions are asked. If we can stop attempting to make everything clear through our own words and allow the students to guide us, we are modeling simplicity of thought that will serve us all well.

I had an exercise instructor who guided the class with clear and simple instructions. He explained complex movements in few words and included times of silence in his teaching. I have also worked with exercise instructors who seem to be talking all the time. They give instructions two or three different ways, offer encouragement constantly, and generally fill up any silence with further explanations. Having to focus so carefully on the instructor's words, I had no opportunity to listen to my own body. As we simplify our teaching, our students have time for reflection and can integrate their learning into their lives.

PATIENCE

If letting go is at the heart of simplicity, slowing down is central to the gift of patience. We live in a culture that is always rushing. Drivers get impatient with the car in front of them traveling at the speed limit. Pedestrians run across the street, often going against the light. Students dash between classes. Along with the actual rushing, an attitude of urgency is rife in the culture. Urgency can be contagious; if we are not careful, we can become as urgent as those around us. By slowing down and looking closely at what is happening, we can determine whether a situation is truly urgent or whether there is actually no rush at all.

The value of patience and slowing down is rarely honored. In fact, many of us are unhappy about having to slow down as a result of aging. I hear other elders complaining, "I just can't do as much as I used to," "I get tired much more easily than before, even without a full day's work," "Sometimes I need a nap in the middle of the day."

What if we were to experience slowing down and the patience that follows as one of our treasures, no matter what our age? Remember Joey, the preschool Montessori teacher who discovered he had to curb his enthusiasm when in the classroom as he watched and waited for the young children to find their way? What a treasure for these youngsters, being allowed to move at their own pace, rather than being hurried through a learning experience.

When teachers are patient, we open the space for students to explore learning in their own way and at their own rate. Albert Einstein wrote about teaching, "I never teach my pupils. I only attempt to provide the conditions in which they can learn."[6] To provide such space takes patience as we wait for students to risk stepping forward into their own learning. They need to know we

> When teachers are patient we open the space for students to explore learning in their own way and at their own rate.

are supporting their slow progress. When I'm leading spiritual retreats, I tell participants there is only one rule for our time together: "No rushing!" A collective sigh goes up from the group and they settle into the present moment. They realize the spirit cannot be rushed. By being patient, I am drawing forth their own patience.

COMPASSION

Compassion is surely not the same as pity, sympathy, or even empathy, although, according to Buddhist teacher Sharon Salzburg, empathy is what leads us to true compassion. She explains that feeling empathy for others does not mean we know what they feel, but it allows us to enter into their experience, thus putting us in touch with similar feelings within our own hearts.[7]

When someone is weeping with loneliness, we may try to comfort her by saying we know what she is feeling. But this is disrespectful. We can never know another's feelings, for everyone experiences loneliness differently. However, if I let the other person's pain trigger my own experience of loss and loneliness, I can empathize with her. I still don't know what she is feeling, but I call up my own feelings from my earlier experiences of loss. Then I can offer compassion.

I believe this understanding of compassion is important for teachers, for we are often in relationship with students whose feelings and behaviors stem from experiences that have never been part of our lives. When we are not familiar with their lives and have little understanding of how they feel, we often wonder how compassionate we can be. Think of a student coming to school the day after her brother has been shot in an incident of gang violence. We may not know how she feels, but we can allow her grief and anger to touch that place inside us that resonates with her pain. We may then be able to offer her an authentic compassionate response.

In the story of Joey standing on the top of the slide, I like to imagine that empathy and compassion allowed his mother to honor his unhappiness with his preschool, and his insistence that she find him another placement. She couldn't know just what Joey was feeling, but somehow his passion stirred something within her. Maybe she remembered what it was like to feel stuck someplace that made her miserable. Her compassion allowed her to understand that Joey's request from the top of the slide was not a form of blackmail but rather a longing of his heart to be free.

LIBERATION

"The truth will set you free," proclaims the Christian scriptures (John 8:32). I think we have all had that experience in some area of our lives, although we often do not want to hear that truth. After listening for many weeks to a friend sharing what was happening in her marriage, I said to her hesitantly, "It sounds to me as if you are being emotionally abused." She denied it and grew defensive, but later told me that my naming her experience as abuse opened her eyes and heart to what was happening. She was then free to take action.

New insights can set us free from old ways of thinking or believing. I remember the first time I heard God referred to as She. I was amazed at how wrong that felt, but it jarred me into thinking more deeply about my images of God. I realized that I had been trapped by the cultural assumption of the maleness of God. The nature of God still remains a mystery to me, but the truth that was revealed to me was an opening of possibilities to explore and experience many images. I was freed from a narrow understanding of the nature of God that I didn't even know I was holding on to.

> New insights can set us free from old ways of thinking or believing.

Many of us, and probably most of our students, experience liberation as synonymous with autonomy and independence. However, liberation is more complex than simply the freedom *from* restrictions; we must also ask what we are being freed *for*. Asking and reflecting on this question can lead us to develop the skills, habits, virtues, and disciplines to live rich and meaningful lives.

This is a crucial question for teachers as we offer the possibility of freedom to our students. We need to model in our own lives not only our struggle for freedom from those things that bind us but also what kind of life that liberation allows us to live. Jessica Yeager, who is homeschooling her children, freed herself and her daughters from what she saw as a divisive and limiting school environment. In doing so, she took on the hard work and discipline of providing her children an integrated curriculum that reflected her values.

Any institution where you work will have requirements you would rather not adhere to. Maybe you resist standardized testing, a class schedule that makes no sense to you, expectations to attend certain meetings, or the new IT program that must be mastered. You would like to be free from those demands so that you could then teach with more integrity. You may see the restrictions as keeping you from your authentic self. You may imagine that breaking through the external barriers will allow you the freedom to teach in new and creative ways. Reflecting on the possibilities of what you might be freed *for* is important, but sometimes you may realize that you can do nothing about those rules and regulations. When you cannot be liberated from external restrictions, you can turn your attention to the deeper freedom that comes from remembering you always have a choice of how to be and teach within those limits. This is a treasure you can bring your students when you live with this ultimate freedom—to be who you are no matter what the circumstances.

LOVE

Love is not just a feeling; it is a way of being in the world. Love is what gives us the courage to take risks, to overcome major obstacles in the teaching-learning process. Garret Keizer sees the love of students as a primary, even indispensable, motivation in teachers, especially if you can add, "I love their parents, too." He believes that the true revolutionary is guided by a great feeling of love, and so is the true teacher. "It has become a kind of mantra for me," he writes, "*I need to love*."[8]

Keizer added love of parents to the capacity to love our students and in Chapter 3 we examined how love of the subjects we are teaching affects the teaching-learning process. Kristin Waters, the Denver high school principal, took it even further when I asked her about the joy and delight she finds in her teaching role. Although she acknowledged the frustrations and heartaches inherent in the teaching life, she said that when she stepped back and looked at the big picture, beyond the details claiming her attention, she was simply able to love it all.

GRATITUDE

Heidi Boerstler, the business school professor, began the story of her call to teach with an expression of deep gratitude for her second-grade teacher who took her regularly to an orphanage to play with a classmate. When Heidi asked why she had been selected for this experience, her teacher replied, "I believe you can do good in the world, and I want you to realize this right now." That early affirmation has been a deep influence as Heidi followed call after call until arriving at her deepest calling—to introduce business school students to the power of the spirit moving in their lives.

Heidi is filled with gratitude, not only for the opportunities she has been given but also for the small things in life and the day-to-day challenges of her vocation. "I try to see all the people I work with through the eyes of a grateful heart," she said. "I don't want to make assumptions about who they are and what they want. I try to remember that they are unique and their own wisdom will guide them. I give thanks for their presence in my teaching life and am grateful for what they teach me."

I believe that a grateful heart is the natural response to recognizing the treasures we have been exploring. Both patience and simplicity draw us toward a wider view of ourselves and the world and give us the time and space to open our hearts in gratitude. By sitting silently and patiently with a student, letting go of our expectations, and waiting for whatever is trying to come forth, we can become grateful for the opportunity to be with another in such a sacred place.

Experiences of liberation lead to gratefulness. Our gratitude can sometimes feel so dramatic that we might exclaim, "Thanks be to God!" However, when we are led to truth through painful seeing, our gratitude may take a while to arrive. Yet if we do our inner work, arrive it will. A woman at a dinner party casually told me she had lost her job six months ago. "It was a terrible experience," she said. "I had to look at and feel the shame of inadequacy. I had to examine my life plans and my expectations for living a full life. That was not easy, but what I have discovered is a new experience of life's riches. I am now grateful for the firing, for I never would have had the courage to leave that position on my own."

I believe that love and gratitude are intertwined. When I am grateful, I am better able to express and receive love. When I offer love to another, I am often motivated by gratitude, and suffused with gratefulness when my love is received. Gratitude may open my heart, allowing me to receive the gift of love from another. All these treasures combine to help us not just feel gratitude for various things, but also to live life with a grateful heart. That way of being was expressed eloquently and simply when Kristin Waters exclaimed about her experience of teaching, "I love it all!"

WISDOM

Wisdom seems to defy description, but we tend to know it when we see or hear it. We are acutely aware of the wisdom and the accompanying humility we experience in others. Being in their presence often gives rise to the longing to possess such wisdom for ourselves, and we begin to search for it, always believing wisdom lies somewhere beyond us. Poet Mark Nepo describes the outcome of his search: "I wanted to become wise, but after much travel and study, it was during my bedridden days with cancer that I realized I was already wise. I just didn't know the language of my wisdom."[9]

I don't think that Nepo is referring to words when he writes of the "language of wisdom." I believe he is implying that one's wisdom is not expressed through words but rather through the language of being. Who he is and how he lives are the expression of his wisdom. Therefore, we cannot find wisdom beyond ourselves or teach another how to be wise, but we can create the space for our wisdom and the wisdom of others to be revealed.

In the Zen Buddhist tradition it is believed that teachers cannot teach their students how to wake up; they can only provide the wings of awakening.[10] I imagine this beautiful phrase applies to wisdom as well as awakening. In fact, I think these words are synonymous. As teachers, we need to recognize that teaching the wings of awakening is what the sacred art of teaching is all about. No matter what our subject matter, the age of our students, or the number of students we are responsible for, we are offering them all the wings of awareness. And that is truly the subject of this book.

I have offered examples of teachers building strong relationships with their students and providing a safe place for them to discover their inner teachers. The stories present the possibility that our relationship with our subject matter and the language we use in our teaching can release a student's inner wisdom. As we claim our own authority, we model for our students that they, too, can claim their authority from inside. These last two chapters have helped us to see how teachers' inner work frees them to grow into themselves, thus shining light on the shadows and bringing forth their own unique treasures.

As we learn the language of our own wisdom and provide the wings of awareness for our students, we recognize profound truth in the words of Vietnamese Buddhist monk Thich Nhat Hanh that "our own life has to be our message."[11]

Looking Inward, Going Deeper

1. How do your ancestors and your history affect who you are and who you have become? What threads and themes do you see running through the generations?

2. When have your teaching experiences been transformative, not only in your behavior but also in your deepest being? How has teaching contributed to making you who you are today?

3. Lao-Tzu wrote that he only had three things to teach— simplicity, patience, and compassion. What three words would complete this saying for you? What are your greatest treasures?

ACKNOWLEDGMENTS

At the heart of this book are the experiences and stories of both teachers and students. I am grateful to all of them for their willingness to share their lives in this way. Peter Baer, Heidi Boerstler, Joey Chernila, Steve Replogle, Peter Schneider, Mark Sisun, Erika Walker, Kristin Waters, Dana Wilbanks, and Jessica Yeager graciously agreed to be interviewed and I came away from each of these conversations with a deeper understanding of the teaching vocation.

The other stories come from my own life and from teachers and students who have talked with me about their teaching and learning experiences in casual conversations over many years. I have tried to be faithful to all the stories, although I am sure the passage of time has made complete accuracy impossible.

Special thanks to Emily Wichland, vice president of Editorial and Production at SkyLight Paths Publishing, who invited me to submit a proposal for this book and then shepherded me through the creative process with wisdom and grace. The whole staff at SkyLight Paths contributed their wonderful skills of design, editing, and production to bring this book to completion. I could not have asked for a more creative team.

My husband, Jim Laurie, has been my first reader and a great source of encouragement throughout this process. I am deeply grateful. Paul and Jamie Laurie, my stepsons, show up in these pages, as they do in most of my writing and teaching. I appreciate their good humor with my telling stories about them. They had no idea this would be happening when I joined this family almost thirty years ago.

There is no way to express my thanks to the many students I have encountered over the years. They have taught me much of what I know about teaching by their willingness to challenge me with questions, offer new ideas, confront and test me, as well as offering appreciation for the work of learning and teaching we have done together. I began this book with my dedication to them and now end with heartfelt gratitude.

NOTES

INTRODUCTION

1. Gilbert Highet, *The Art of Teaching* (New York: Alfred A. Knopf, 1951), viii.

2. Joseph Campbell, *Reflections on the Art of Living: A Joseph Campbell Companion*, ed. Diane K. Osbon (New York: Harper Perennial, 1995).

3. Garret Keizer, *Getting Schooled: The Reeducation of an American Teacher* (New York: Henry Holt and Company, 2014), 249.

1. CALLED TO TEACH: DISCOVERING OUR VOCATION

1. James Hollis, *Finding Meaning in the Second Half of Life: How to Finally, Really Grow Up* (New York: Gotham Books, 2005), 149.

2. Adyashanti, *Resurrecting Jesus: Embodying the Spirit of a Revolutionary Mystic* (Boulder, CO: Sounds True, Inc., 2014), 61.

3. Joan Chittister, *Following the Path: The Search for a Life of Passion, Purpose, and Joy* (New York: Random House, Inc., 2012), 81.

4. Keizer, *Getting Schooled*, 3.

5. Shirley Hershey Showalter, *Blush: A Mennonite Girl Meets a Glittering World* (Harrisonburg, VA: Herald Press, 2013), 233.

6. Chittister, *Following the Path*, 152–53.

2. ENGAGING OUR STUDENTS AND COLLEAGUES: RESPECT, CHALLENGE, AND KINDNESS

1. Imam Jamal Rahman, *Sacred Laughter of the Sufis: Awakening the Soul with the Mulla's Comic Teaching Stories & Other Islamic Wisdom* (Woodstock, VT: SkyLight Paths, 2014), 115.

2. Lynn W. Huber, *Revelations on the Road: A Pilgrim Journey* (Boulder, CO: Woven Word Press, 2003), 30–31.

3. Parker J. Palmer, *The Courage to Teach: Exploring the Inner Landscape of a Teacher's Life* (San Francisco: Jossey-Bass, 1998), 30.

4. David Stricklin, interviewer, *Oral Memoirs of Paul and Kitty Baker* (Waco, TX: Baylor University Institute of Oral History, 1997), 44.

5. Howard Gardner, *Frames of Mind: The Theory of Multiple Intelligences* (New York: Basic Books, 1983).

6. Howard Gardner, *Multiple Intelligences: New Horizons* (New York: Basic Books, 2006), 18–21.

7. Stricklin, *Oral Memoirs of Paul and Kitty Baker*, 43.

8. For ideas for teaching through multiple intelligences, see Linda C. Campbell and Bruce Campbell, *Teaching and Learning through Multiple Intelligences*, 3rd ed. (New York: Basic Books, 2003).

9. Alix Spiegel, "Why Eastern and Western Cultures Tackle Learning Differently," *NPR Morning Edition* (September 2, 2013).

10. Ibid.

11. Henri J. M. Nouwen, *Reaching Out: The Three Movements of the Spiritual Life* (Garden City, NY: Doubleday & Company, Inc., 1975), 58–63.

12. Ibid., 70.

13. Keizer, *Getting Schooled*, 165.

14. Bob Smietana, "Agents of Grit and Grace," *Sojourner* (September–October 2014): 28.

15. Steven Dubner, "The Economist's Guide to Parenting," New Freakonomics Radio Podcast (August 17, 2011).

16. Highet, *The Art of Teaching*, 64–65.

17. Nouwen, *Reaching Out*, 63.

3. LOVE OF SUBJECT, LOVE OF LEARNING: COMMUNICATING EXCITEMENT AND WONDER

1. Rahman, *Sacred Laughter of the Sufis*, 116–17.

2. Palmer, *The Courage to Teach*, 100–1.

3. Ibid., 103.

4. Wayne Whitson Floyd, "Ten Lessons about Being a Learner-Centered Teacher, " https://albanroundtable.wordpress.com/2009/07/06/resources (accessed December 2014).

5. Highet, *The Art of Teaching*, 48–49.

6. Floyd, "Ten Lessons."

4. USING SACRED LANGUAGE: TELLING STORIES, ASKING QUESTIONS, AND LISTENING WELL

1. Eugene Peterson, *The Contemplative Pastor: Returning to the Art of Spiritual Direction* (Dallas: Word Publishing, 1989), 98–99.

2. Barbara Brown Taylor, *When God Is Silent* (Boston: Cowley Publications, 1998), 101.

3. Native American elder Sa'k'ej Hendersong, in Mark Nepo, *The Book of Awakening* (San Francisco: Conti Press, 2000), 353.

4. Marilynne Robinson, "Our Stories and the Theatre of Awe," *Santa Clara Magazine* (Summer 2014): 39.

5. Rainer Maria Rilke, "Letters to a Young Poet" (Mineola, NY: Dover Publications, 2012).

5. CLAIMING OUR AUTHORITY BY LETTING GO OF CONTROL

1. Henri J. M. Nouwen, *Bread for the Journey: A Daybook of Wisdom and Faith* (New York: HarperCollins, 1997), 12.

2. Viktor E. Frankl, *Man's Search for Meaning: An Introduction to Logotherapy* (New York: Simon & Schuster, Inc., 1963).

6. ATTENDING TO OUR INNER LANDSCAPE: SEEING, EMBRACING, AND TRANSFORMING OUR SHADOWS

1. Thomas Huxley, to Charles Kingsley, September 23, 1860, in "T. H. Huxley Letters and Diary 1860," http://aleph0.clark.edu/huxley/letters/60.html (accessed January 13, 2015).

2. Kathleen Norris, *Amazing Grace: A Vocabulary of Faith* (New York: Riverhead Books, 1998), 55.

3. Ibid.

4. Ibid.

5. Shunryu Suzuki, *Zen Mind, Beginner's Mind* (New York: Weatherhill, 1970), 21.

6. Palmer, *The Courage to Teach*, 112.

7. Br. David Steindl-Rast, *Gratefulness, the Heart of Prayer: An Approach to Life in Fullness* (New York: Paulist Press, 1984), 22.

8. Abraham Joshua Heschel, *Man Is Not Alone: A Philosophy of Religion* (New York: Farrar Straus and Giroux, 1951), 11.

9. Palmer, *The Courage to Teach*, 2.

10. Keizer, *Getting Schooled*, 149.

11. Palmer, *The Courage to Teach*, 3.

7. TEACHING WHO WE ARE: HONORING OUR UNIQUE GIFTS

1. Vincent Harding and Daisaku Ikeda, *America Will Be! Conversations on Hope, Freedom, and Democracy* (Cambridge, MA: Dialogue Path Press, 2013), 64.

2. Ibid., 65.

3. Keizer, *Getting Schooled*, 1.

4. Lao-Tzu, in Nepo, *The Book of Awakening*, 223.

5. Winston Churchill, in Nepo, *The Book of Awakening*, 365.

6. Albert Einstein, www.goodreads.com/quotes (accessed September 2014).

7. Sharon Salzburg, Zencare Podcasts, www.zencare.org/podcasts/zencare_podcasts.xml (accessed January 5, 2011).

8. Keizer, *Getting Schooled*, 191–92.

9. Nepo, *The Book of Awakening*, 285.

10. Roshi Joan Halifax, Plenary Presentation, Spiritual Directors International Conference, Santa Fe, NM, April 27, 2014.

11. Thich Nhat Hanh, *The World We Have: A Buddhist Approach to Peace and Ecology* (Berkeley, CA: Parallax Press, 2008).

SUGGESTIONS FOR FURTHER READING

Chittister, Joan. *Following the Path: The Search for a Life of Passion, Purpose, and Joy.* New York: Random House, Inc., 2012.

Doughty, Steve. *To Walk in Integrity: Spiritual Leadership in Times of Crisis.* Nashville: The Upper Room, 2004.

Hahn, Celia Allison. *Growing in Authority, Relinquishing Control: A New Approach to Faithful Leadership.* Herndon, VA: The Alban Institute, 1994.

Harnden, Philip. *Journeys of Simplicity: Traveling Light with Thomas Merton, Basho, Edward Abbey, Annie Dillard, and Others.* Woodstock, VT: SkyLight Paths, 2003.

Heider, John. *The Tao of Leadership: Lao Tzu's Tao Te Ching Adapted for a New Age.* Atlanta: Humanics New Age, 1985.

Highet, Gilbert. *The Art of Teaching.* New York: Random House, 1950.

Keizer, Garret. *Getting Schooled: The Reeducation of an American Teacher.* New York: Henry Holt and Company, 2014.

Lindahl, Kay. *The Sacred Art of Listening: Forty Reflections for Cultivating a Spiritual Practice.* Woodstock, VT: SkyLight Paths, 2002.

Moore, Mary Elizabeth Mullino. *Teaching as a Sacramental Act.* Cleveland: The Pilgrim Press, 2004.

Nepo, Mark. *The Book of Awakening: Having the Life You Want by Being Present to the Life You Have.* San Francisco: Conti Press, 2000.

———. *The Exquisite Risk: Daring to Live an Authentic Life.* New York: Three Rivers Press, 2005.

Nouwen, Henri J. M. *Bread for the Journey: A Daybook of Wisdom and Faith.* New York: HarperCollins, 1997.

———. *Reaching Out: The Three Movements of the Spiritual Life.* Garden City, NY: Doubleday & Company, 1975.

Palmer, Parker J. *The Courage to Teach: Exploring the Inner Landscape of a Teacher's Life.* San Francisco: Jossey-Bass, 1998.

Schirch, Lisa, and David Campt. *The Little Book of Dialogue for Difficult Subjects: A Practical, Hands-On Guide.* Intercourse, PA: Good Books, 2007.

Shapiro, Rami. *The Sacred Art of Lovingkindness: Preparing to Practice.* Woodstock, VT: SkyLight Paths, 2006.

Steindl-Rast, David. *Gratefulness, the Heart of Prayer: An Approach to Life in Fullness.* New York: Paulist Press, 1984.

Vennard, Jane. *Fully Awake and Truly Alive: Spiritual Practices to Nurture Your Soul.* Woodstock, VT: SkyLight Paths, 2013.

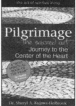

About SKYLIGHT PATHS Publishing

SkyLight Paths Publishing is creating a place where people of different spiritual traditions come together for challenge and inspiration, a place where we can help each other understand the mystery that lies at the heart of our existence.

Through spirituality, our religious beliefs are increasingly becoming a part of our lives—rather than *apart* from our lives. While many of us may be more interested than ever in spiritual growth, we may be less firmly planted in traditional religion. Yet, we do want to deepen our relationship to the sacred, to learn from our own as well as from other faith traditions, and to practice in new ways.

SkyLight Paths sees both believers and seekers as a community that increasingly transcends traditional boundaries of religion and denomination—people wanting to learn from each other, *walking together, finding the way*.

For your information and convenience, at the back of this book we have provided a list of other SkyLight Paths books you might find interesting and useful. They cover the following subjects:

Buddhism / Zen	Gnosticism	Poetry
Catholicism	Hinduism / Vedanta	Prayer
Chaplaincy		Religious Etiquette
Children's Books	Inspiration	Retirement & Later-
Christianity	Islam / Sufism	Life Spirituality
Comparative Religion	Judaism	Spiritual Biography
	Meditation	Spiritual Direction
Earth-Based Spirituality	Mindfulness	Spirituality
	Monasticism	Women's Interest
Enneagram	Mysticism	Worship
Global Spiritual Perspectives	Personal Growth	

Or phone, fax, mail or email to: SKYLIGHT PATHS Publishing
Sunset Farm Offices, Route 4 • P.O. Box 237 • Woodstock, Vermont 05091
Tel: (802) 457-4000 • Fax: (802) 457-4004 • www.skylightpaths.com
Credit card orders: (800) 962-4544 (8:30AM–5:30PM EST Monday–Friday)
Generous discounts on quantity orders. SATISFACTION GUARANTEED. Prices subject to change.

**For more information about each book,
visit our website at www.skylightpaths.com.**